6th grd

Dearest
I am so very happy
that you are "colorblind" and
that you never "judge a book by
its cover" (pardon the clichés). You
always get to know people
from the inside out — never, never
stop being so nonjudgemental, it is a
precious quality as well as a
precious commodity. Always fight
for what's "right," no matter how
unpopular it seems. I already
know you will, your my daughter!
          I love you
          Momma

STUDENTS ON

JIM CROW, CIVIL RIGHTS, *BROWN,* AND ME

A MEMOIR BY
John A. Stokes
with Lois Wolfe, Ph.D.
and Herman J. Viola, Ph.D.

NATIONAL GEOGRAPHIC

WASHINGTON, D.C.

FOR MAMA AND DADDY, WHO INSTILLED THE VALUES
IN ME THAT HAVE MADE ME THE MAN THAT I AM TODAY.
MAY THEY REST IN PEACE.
—J.A.S.

FOR MY MOM, GERRY MCEWUEN ELLIS, WHO TAUGHT ME TO RESPECT
PEOPLE OF ALL RACES, CREEDS, AND RELIGIONS
—L.W.

ACKNOWLEDGMENTS

Gratitude is extended to the following people: Herman Viola, Suzanne Fonda, and Nancy Feresten, for their commitment to bringing this struggle for equality and justice to print so that all people may be enlightened about this critical period of our nation's history; my wife, Mildred New Stokes, for her patience and understanding as I labored through this project; my daughter, Courtney Wolfe Rhymer, for her constant love and belief in me; all the students who walked out with us on 23 April 1951, I thank you again; the NAACP and its cadre of lawyers for taking our case; Dr. Cheryl Brown Henderson for her continuing support; Ed Peeples and Mary Harmon for their input, feedback, and support throughout this endeavor; Kimberly Lewis and Sylvia Burch for their hours of transcriptions; all our family and friends too numerous to name individually who gave their continued support; and all the people who have been involved, who are now involved, or who will be involved in struggles for equality and justice for all peoples. Keep on keeping on!

For information about special discounts for bulk purchases, please contact
National Geographic Books Special Sales: ngspecsales@ngs.org

For rights or permissions inquiries, please contact
National Geographic Books Subsidiary Rights: ngbookrights@ngs.org

Cover design by Bea Jackson. Interior design by David M. Seager and Melissa Brown
Fonts: myriad pro, Felt Tip, and Mrs. Eaves

LIBRARY OF CONGRESS CATALOGING-IN-PUBLICATION DATA

Stokes, John A., 1931-
   Students on strike : Jim crow, civil rights, *Brown*, and me / a memoir by John A. Stokes with Lois Wolfe, Ph.D., and Herman J. Viola Ph.D.
   p. cm.
   Includes bibliographical references and index.
   ISBN 978-1-4263-0153-7 (trade : alk. paper)
   ISBN 978-1-4263-0154-4 (library : alk. paper)
1. African American students—Southern States—History. 2. Segregation in education—Southern States—History. 3. School environment—Southern States—History. I. Wolfe, Lois, 1952- II. Viola, Herman J. III. Title.
LC2731.S76 2008
371.829'96073075—dc22

        2007034677

Front cover: Strike leader John A. Stokes looks out over a group of the students and parents whose names appeared as plaintiffs in a lawsuit that sought to end segregated schools in Prince Edward County, Virginia. Taken on the steps of the capitol in Richmond, the photograph shows the author in the front row, second from the left. Overhead is a portion of a poster from the student strike at Robert Russa Moton High School.

Printed in the United States of America

CONTENTS

Note from the Author 5

CHAPTER 1   **FEAR MAKES ME HIDE** 7

CHAPTER 2   **GROWING UP RICH IN SPIRIT** 14

CHAPTER 3   **SCHOOL DAYS** 18

CHAPTER 4   **LIFE IN THE JIM CROW SOUTH** 22

CHAPTER 5   **BEATING THE SYSTEM** 30

CHAPTER 6   **LESSONS FROM NED** 33

CHAPTER 7   **THE SKY DID NOT FALL** 38

CHAPTER 8   **SEPARATE BUT NEVER EQUAL** 44

CHAPTER 9   **OUR MANHATTAN PROJECT** 54

CHAPTER 10   **THERE'S A RIOT AT THE SCHOOL** 63

CHAPTER 11   **TAKING CARE OF BUSINESS** 71

CHAPTER 12   **DON'T GIVE UP** 79

CHAPTER 13   **UNCHARTED WATERS** 86

CHAPTER 14   **A SKITTISH NIGHT** 93

CHAPTER 15   **COVER ME** 101

CHAPTER 16   ***DAVIS V. COUNTY SCHOOL BOARD OF PRINCE EDWARD COUNTY*** 105

CHAPTER 17   **MASSIVE RESISTANCE** 112

AFTERWORD   **STANDING ON SHOULDERS** 118

Bibliography 126

Resources 127

Not everything that is faced can be changed.
But nothing can be changed until it is faced.

—James Baldwin

NOTE FROM THE AUTHOR

For you to fully understand what you are about to read, you must try to imagine what it would be like to live in a United States with a social structure very different from today's society, where there is concern for everyone's civil rights. You must try to put yourself in my shoes or those of my twin sister, Carrie, or any of the students who attended Robert Russa Moton High School in 1951, or any of the black people who lived in just about any southern state. What happened in Prince Edward County, Virginia, was before the time of Rosa Parks, Martin Luther King, Jr., Little Rock, or just about any other big civil rights event that you have studied in school. It was the time when there were laws upheld by the U.S. Constitution that made it legal to separate the races. It was a time when "blacks" or "African Americans" were known as "Negroes" or "coloreds," when segregation was the rule, and when integration was a new and little-practiced concept. Welcome to the world of Jim Crow. Read on to find out how a bunch of high school students pitted their wits against the white power structure. See how—against all odds— these students joined forces with others to gain their rights and the rights for all people as human beings in American society by becoming part of a lawsuit that led to the U.S. Supreme Court decision that marked the beginning of the end of segregation in America.

CHAPTER 1

FEAR MAKES ME HIDE

I am a colored boy. I am 12 years old, and I am hiding among the bushes and trees alongside the highway until the slow-moving car travels past me. No, I have not committed any crime, I am not a fugitive, and I am not running away from home. But I did run, and now I am hiding. It is after dark on this very hot and humid evening in rural Virginia. My entire body is covered in sweat. My clothes are sticking to me. In my haste to get away, I hit a barbed wire fence. The barbs ripped through my pants and tore holes in my skin. I feel the hot blood trickling down my legs and soaking my pants.

Whenever and wherever colored children are walking after dark, we are taught to take cover in ditches and gullies, behind bushes and trees, in culverts, or in any safe hiding place as soon as we hear or see a car approaching us from the front or the rear. I have hidden many, many times. But this night is different. It is one of those nights that the old folks would describe as "being on the dark side of the moon."

The road is U.S. Route 15, which meanders through the Piedmont area of Virginia on its long journey between Canada and South Carolina. Not much traffic passes here at night, and this car is the very first I've seen since I left Farmville to walk the four and a half miles home. Mr. Hall, our Boy Scout leader and principal of my elementary school, dismissed us from the Scout meeting long before dark, but instead of hurrying home, I slipped into downtown Farmville to go to the movies with some other kids. We were just having too much fun to keep track of the time. Now I was paying the price.

Did I wait too long before running into the thickets? Did the people in the car see me before I saw them? Are they really slowing down? Are they going to stop? Are they going to hurt me?

My eyes have adjusted to the darkness. I thought that I was doing well, but I make a terrible mistake. I look at the approaching car lights instead of looking away. Now my eyes are blinded. Mama and Daddy have taught me better. "Keep your eyes focused toward the darkness, not the light, and you will be able to see. If necessary, turn your back to the oncoming lights until you get your bearings. A headlight will blind you, especially on a moonless night," they have always warned us. At least I had obeyed Mama and Daddy as far as clothing was concerned. I had on all dark clothes, although it was hot as blazes. Dark clothing enabled us to "disappear" at night, especially on moonless nights like this one.

This is such an isolated area. Houses and people are so very far apart that at times it appears as if it is a "no-man's land." This is why anyone wanting to do harm to colored people here doesn't have to worry much about getting caught.

During this time in the South, it is not unusual for colored boys and girls to be taunted, hurt, and even killed, especially if they are caught alone at night. The white authorities blame us. They ask, "Just why are you all out at this time of night anyhow?" We know we can never get fair treatment from the police. A colored person can't win a case in court. It is our words against theirs. You see, all law enforcement officers and elected officials are white. We suspect most of them are part of the dreaded Ku

Klux Klan, who harass and kill colored people whenever they can. If they are not part of the Klan, they support them in their actions against colored people.

As these thoughts run through my mind, I notice something moving between the road and me. What in the world is over there? My mind starts spinning. What if it's a snake? I am scared to death of snakes, but tonight I would rather take a chance with a snake than have an encounter with white people.

I know the car has white people in it because local black folks don't travel at this time of night except in an extreme emergency. Besides, the car is too new to belong to any local black people. We boys know the sounds of most of the cars around here and whether they belong to blacks or whites. In fact, we even sometimes play guessing games. With our eyes closed, we try to identify who owns a passing car.

My mind snaps back to my immediate problem. My heart feels as if it is coming out of my chest. It is pounding. The more I try to breathe quietly, the louder it seems. My entire body is trembling. I have goose pimples all over. I am thinking, "The Devil is getting me now because I disobeyed Mama and Daddy." Their orders were as clear as day: "Come home as soon as Mr. Hall dismisses you."

How could I have been so stupid? I am trapped between the road and the barbed wire fence that surrounds the pasture where Mr. Dunnington's dairy cattle graze. I hear the animals breathing and stirring. If I try to crawl under the fence and run toward home, I will be chased and maybe killed by one of the bulls that Mr. Dunnington keeps in this pasture. My daddy often talks about being between a rock and a hard place. I figure that's where I am right now.

My heart jumps into my mouth as the car crawls to a stop a short distance beyond where I am hiding. It just sits there, idling quietly. Two white men get out. My body freezes. I try to stop breathing, fearful they can hear me. The creature between me and the highway starts to move toward me just as the men get out of the car. It's a cat. When I pick up a stone to throw at it, the cat runs across the highway. The two men point a flashlight in its direction, then shine it back on the car to check the tires or wheels.

Just then another car comes roaring up the road from Farmville. The sound of the juiced-up motor tells me it probably belongs to a bootlegger. That's a person who makes and sells illegal whiskey known as moonshine. These people use these high-powered machines so they can outrun police cars. No one else would have a motor like that. There are lots of moonshine operators around here. The local folks call the drivers "Shine Runners" or just "Runners." They are very dangerous. They trust no one, and they will hurt anyone who threatens their business. We learn to stay out of their way.

This car screeches to a stop. The driver gets out and joins the two other men. After what seems like an eternity, they all get back in their cars and drive off. Whew! I hear the cattle grazing gently to my left as I move out of my hiding place among the trees and bushes. My heartbeat has slowed down, the goose pimples are gone, and I gradually regain my composure. As I run along the highway toward home, I hear the owls, the crickets, the tree frogs, and the other night creatures, but my eyes and ears are peeled for humans—white ones. My entire body is ready for action.

When I reach our farm, I give a low whistling sound to alert our dogs that I'm home. Ring explodes from his usual guard place and runs to the highway to meet me. He circles me and tries to jump on me, then licks my hand and falls to the ground, hoping I will scratch him. I pat his head and move toward the house. I greet the other dogs and then enter through the back door.

Boy, am I glad to be home! Mama and Daddy keep farm hours, so they are already in bed. I very softly let them know that I'm home. As I head up the steps to my room, I hear them resume their snoring. Breathing a double sigh of relief, I pray to God and thank him that I made it home safe. I take an Epsom salt bath to rid my body of any chiggers I may have picked up in the bushes. I wash my cuts with hydrogen peroxide, put a coating of BFI antiseptic powder on them, and then cover them with gauze and tape. I do not sleep well tonight. Headlights haunt my dreams.

CHAPTER 2

GROWING UP RICH IN SPIRIT

I was born on December 31, 1931, in Kingsville, Virginia. Kingsville was a small community located near Farmville in Prince Edward County, about 70 miles southwest of Richmond. To picture the location of Prince Edward County, simply think of the geographic center of Virginia. I had three older brothers (Clem, Howard, and Leslie), one older sister (Martha), and a twin sister (Carrie). The six of us lived with our parents on a small farm.

We were a close-knit family. My mother, Alice, worked in the laundry at Longwood College, in Farmville, and washed and ironed clothes for students at nearby Hampden-Sydney College, too. She also cooked and cleaned for white people and took care of their children. My father, Luther, was a truck farmer. That meant my daddy raised produce that he took to market. Just like most truck farmers did back then, our family lived off the land. We relied upon nature and the soil for our existence, something that would be hard for any family to do nowadays. We grew vegetables, such as squash, peppers, string beans, butter beans, sweet peas, corn, and collard greens; root crops, such as potatoes and onions; and fruits, such as tomatoes, watermelons, and cantaloupes. We also raised hogs that we slaughtered, then cleaned the meat, smoked it, packed it, and stored it to eat during the wintertime.

Physically sound, mentally awake, and morally straight; we lived by those rules. My siblings and I were never idle. We always had chores to do. Some were inside duties, and some were outside duties. Some, like milking cows on a neighbor's farm every morning and evening or helping farmers with their harvests, I got paid for. Others I did to help out at home.

Growing up, we did not have distractions such as television and computers. I think Carrie and I were in high school before our family got a television. We did have a radio, and we would listen to the news and other programs. And we had lots of books. Even though Daddy only went to school through the third grade and Mama went through the fifth grade, they understood the importance of reading.

Daddy read newspapers every chance he got, usually three papers every day: The *Farmville Herald,* the *Richmond Times-Dispatch,* and the *Richmond News Leader.* He also read the *Richmond Afro-American,* which was available weekly in our area. My father critiqued and analyzed these newspapers and had us do the same. I was proud of his ability to interpret the news stories. Even as a child, I thought that this particular ability was a great achievement for someone who had only completed the third grade. Through Daddy's guidance, we all learned how to think critically and how to reason.

Mama was a Bible scholar and could quote verses like a preacher. I called her our family's Bible warrior. No matter where we were going each day—whether to work in the fields or to study at school—Mama would give us a Bible verse to think about and follow. She helped all of us to feel a sense of peace, knowing that we could face anything that might come our way.

We knew that our parents loved us very much, and we loved and respected them for all they did for our family. Despite their own lack of education, Mama and Daddy instilled in each of us a desire to learn. "Knowledge is power" is the message my siblings and I heard over and over. Our parents assured us that, no matter what obstacles came our way, we would achieve our goals. In fact, all the colored children in our community learned at an early age that education was the key to success. We understood the bar was set high for us, and we knew we had to climb up to reach that bar.

CHAPTER 3

SCHOOL DAYS

When my sister Carrie and I started school, just getting there was a challenge. The only public school buses were the ones that took white kids to white schools. So Carrie and I had to walk four and a half miles along the gravel shoulder of U.S. Route 15, one of the busiest highways in the area, to get to Farmville. We walked with our older brothers Howard and Leslie, who went to the high school right next to our elementary school. If we walked too slowly, they would tell us we had to move faster. Then we would break into what our daddy called a dogtrot—something between a walk and a run. The trip wasn't so bad on nice days, but when it was hot or rainy, we were miserable. The worst part was when a bus carrying white kids to school passed us. Sometimes they would spit at us and call us names.

Carrie and I were luckier than our older brothers and sister had been. A couple of months after we started school a bus owned by a colored company started running the route. It didn't go into neighborhoods like most school buses do today. It just ran along the main county roads. We were fortunate that Route 15 ran right past our house. Mama and Daddy paid the owners $1.00 a month (50¢ for each of us) so that Carrie and I could ride on that bus. That may not seem like a lot of money to you, but it was a real sacrifice. We were living during the Depression. Money was hard to come by, and every penny was precious.

Carrie and I were almost nine when we started school. You see, we were supposed to go to Mercy Seat Elementary School, in Hampden-Sydney, just as Howard and Leslie had. But to get there we would have had to walk through a woods, and our parents knew what dangers could lurk there. At age six I wasn't big enough to take care of myself, let alone look after Carrie. We ended up going to school in Farmville, but not until we were old enough to walk along the highway with Howard and Leslie.

Our school was the only elementary school for blacks in all of Prince Edward County that was built of bricks and had running water, indoor toilets, and central heat. Each of the other dozen or so mostly one- or two-room black elementary schools scattered throughout the county *(see map, pages 46–47)* had a wood or coal stove for heat and no indoor water or toilets. Kids and teachers had to use outhouses no matter what the weather. The worst thing about them was the odor. Students could smell them before they ever got near enough to use them. The white power structure—the people who controlled everything and made and enforced all the rules we had to live by—did not have the decency to make sure the toilets were kept clean or to have them filled in when they were full. Then there were the snakes. Often students told how they would see a snake slither away from the outhouse just as they were on their way in.

My friend Jack Jeffers had a hard time understanding why we had to go to different schools and why his school was so much better than mine. Jack was white. His house was not far from ours. Whenever we both had time, he would come over and play. (It was acceptable for black and white kids to do things together so long as they didn't do it in public.) His family had moved to Virginia from Newfoundland, an island off the east coast of Canada. They did not understand why such a division existed between the blacks and whites in their new community. Jack's mother and father taught him that there should be equality and justice for all people. He did not see color; he saw human beings. Jack was sometimes called names by other white kids because he took a stand against the idea that whites were superior to blacks. He often asked me, "Why don't they want you to learn?"

It took me a while to figure out an answer to Jack's question. But eventually I came to realize that by denying us transportation to school and by providing schools that were grossly unequal to the ones white children attended, the white power structure was programming us to fail. This realization would play a pivotal role in the events that would unfold my senior year at Robert Russa Moton High School.

CHAPTER 4

LIFE IN THE JIM CROW SOUTH

o fully appreciate why black schools were so inferior to white schools, why Jack Jeffers was called names by other white kids, and why I was so terrified that night on the highway, you have to understand what life was like in the Jim Crow South. Jim Crow was a derogatory term for a black person that came to refer to all the laws and customs that deprived African Americans of their civil rights and that caused us to be treated as second-class citizens.

When I was growing up in the South, it was against the law for whites and blacks to associate with each other in public. Even if some whites wanted to talk or otherwise socialize with blacks, other whites would attempt to embarrass or make a spectacle of them. Restaurants, movie theaters, buses, and trains either had separate sections for blacks or didn't allow them to enter at all. Blacks couldn't use the same drinking fountains or public bathrooms as whites, and black children had to attend separate schools if they could find a way to even go to school. Blacks were often expected to use rear entrances to homes, not the front door. We knew whose houses had those rules.

Did you ever wonder what it would be like to have to buy shoes and clothes without being able to try them on to see if they fit right? That was standard for blacks in the Jim Crow South. Occasionally a merchant would allow blacks to come in after hours—through the back door, of course—to be fitted for clothes and shoes. My family didn't buy from such people. We felt if we couldn't enter through the front door, then our money would not enter the cash register. Several of the big catalog companies, such as Sears and Roebuck and Montgomery Ward, made a lot of money from blacks at this time because they would allow us to return items through the mail that didn't fit.

There were lots of other rules. Many of them were unspoken, which made it easy for a white person to accuse a black person of not "knowing his or her place." This could mean a severe reprimand, jail time, a beating, or worse. The Ku Klux Klan was active throughout the South, and fear of it was very real among blacks. Money didn't matter in the Jim Crow South. Color came first. As the saying went, "When you are white, you are right; when you are black, stand back."

The Supreme Court, the highest court in the country, made Jim Crow concepts legal and constitutional with its "separate but equal" ruling in a case called *Plessy v. Ferguson* in 1896. This ruling made the segregation (separation) of blacks and whites legal and constitutional so long as the facilities—things like schools, restaurants, restrooms, theaters, means of transportation, and more—provided for both races were deemed equal.

In practice, the concept of "equal" became a matter of interpretation. In the Jim Crow South, "equal" was whatever the whites in power said it was. Rather than creating "separate but equal" facilities, the ruling paved the way for the creation of separate and unequal facilities that made African Americans feel like inferior human beings. It divided the human race and brought out the worst in people. It drove wedges between people who needed each other to survive, and it caused people of the same race to turn against each other. It gave law enforcement officers as well as ordinary citizens reasons to treat blacks unfairly. As a result of the misinterpretation of *Plessy v. Ferguson,* many people, especially in the South, were taken advantage of, threatened, hurt, and even killed without the authorities blinking an eye.

Constantly being made aware of my place was part of my everyday life. A few incidents are as vivid today as they were when they happened 50 years ago.

I used to earn money working at nearby farms. During one summer harvest when I was about 14 or 15, I was working with a white man on a large farm in the Persimmon Tree Fork area not far from my home. We worked together often. He drove the tractor while I minded the combine. The combine was a machine that separated the wheat grain from the stalks, then blew the grain through a chute. At the end of the chute was a platform for the bags that caught the grain. It was my job to tie each bag securely and then hit the trapdoor with my foot to release the loaded bag. Next, I had to guide the bag down the ramp with one hand while holding onto the railing with the other hand, all the while making certain that the bag cleared the back of the combine without tearing, snagging, or spilling any grain. For this hot, tiresome, and difficult job, I was paid 50¢

an hour—the going wage for this sort of work for blacks and whites alike.

We would be in fields at sunup and work until 3 or 4 p.m. We ate lunch around noon and took a water break every two or three hours, depending on how hot it was. The tractor driver had only one water bucket and one dipper, so we had to drink our water from the same dipper when we worked together. Since I was the one who fetched the water, I would drink my water at the spring before filling the bucket and bringing it back to the work area so that he could have a drink—no questions asked.

One day the temperature was in the mid-90s. We had finished a job and were both wringing wet with sweat. To look at me you would think I lived in a dust factory. The sharp, prickly chaff from the grain was sticking into my skin and making me itchy all over. I felt as though I was being attacked by a family of porcupines and all their friends! I was definitely ready to go home. Then I got the bad news. The tractor driver needed me to help him harvest another crop on a farm that I had never been to.

Everything went well until we took our first break. The man who owned the farm invited both of us to his house, where he offered us homemade vanilla ice cream. He gave the driver his share, gave himself his share, and gave me my share. Then he said, "Let's go around front and sit on the porch— out of the sun—and enjoy this."

"Wow!" I thought. "I am going to be out of the sun." As the owner and the driver headed to the front of the house, I was tagging along. The owner of the house stopped dead in his tracks, told the driver to go ahead, and then shouted, "Not you, boy. You take a seat right here on these back steps and eat yours."

I was really hurt, not so much by the owner's words as by the driver. The man who I had eaten lunch with and shared a water dipper with all day long never said a word. He didn't even turn around. He just continued to the front of the house with the owner.

As much as I loved vanilla ice cream, I was so angry I threw my ice cream on the ground. I washed the saucer and the spoon with the water from the faucet at the back of the house, placed them on the back steps, and then walked to the combine, checked the equipment, and climbed into my working position.

"How did you enjoy the ice cream?" the driver asked when he came back.

"I didn't. I threw mine away."

He looked at me funny, started the tractor, and we continued working.

I threw that ice cream away out of defiance. I smiled outwardly and rejoiced inwardly because, in my mind, I had gained a victory over the power structure.

Other situations were more complicated. When I was growing up it was illegal for blacks and whites to get married. White men could associate with black women, young or old, but no black male could ever associate with a white female of any age. I was very aware that I had to be careful about talking to any white girls, even if my mama was taking care of them.

Heather was the daughter of a family Mama worked for occasionally. Once when her parents went on vacation, they asked Mama to stay at their house and look after their children. I was in the kitchen one day while Heather was eating a piece of toast with strawberry jam on it. She tried to get me to take a bite of her toast. When I refused, she reached out and grabbed me, but I managed to pull away. This was a position I had been warned never to be caught in. I ran from the kitchen, out the back door, and into the backyard. She stood in the kitchen door, still eating the piece of toast, and said in a soft voice, "I am not going to bite you. Why did you run? I am not poison, you know."

I knew that Heather was trouble and that I had to distance myself from her at all costs. You see, as a young white girl, she could have endangered my life if I had permitted her to put a piece of her bread in my mouth. If her brother or any other white boy or man had found out about it, that person might have felt that I had stepped over the line and needed to be taught a lesson.

So you see, in the Jim Crow South colored people had to move between two cultures without offending anyone or crossing them in any way. In other words, we had to "walk on eggs." I walked on eggs, and I stayed out of harm's way, even though I would have loved to eat a piece of that toast with strawberry jam.

CHAPTER 5

BEATING THE SYSTEM

Now don't get me wrong. Even though we had to walk on eggs in the Jim Crow South, we would find ways to buck the system. We really enjoyed those moments, like when occasionally some of us passed for white.

At the time I was growing up, Farmville had two movie theaters. The State was for white people only. About a half block up the street was the Lee, which was for both races—each with its own entrance. Whites sat on the first floor, while blacks had to sit in the balcony. Top-rated movies were shown at the State. Second-rate and X-rated movies were shown at the Lee. If blacks wanted to see a decent movie, they had to travel as far as Lynchburg, Richmond, or Washington, D.C.

One night I was in Farmville with two of my high school buddies, William and Harry. We wanted something to eat, but the stores were closed. The only places that were open that had any snacks were the movie theaters, but we knew that the stuff the Lee Theater sold was stale. The State Theater sold fresh treats, but colored kids were not allowed in. That didn't stop Harry.

You see, Harry had such light skin that he could easily pass for white, but he was proud of his black heritage. Whites in our neighborhood knew he was black, so he wasn't permitted to socialize with them, but folks in Farmville didn't know anything about him. That's why Harry was able to get away with things in the city that he couldn't in the country.

Harry had a plan. While William and I waited quietly outside the State, Harry would go inside, buy some goodies, and then hurry back outside. Harry had done this before, and it had worked. Besides, if anything went wrong, we figured we could outrun anyone who tried to chase us. We were all members of the track team.

Harry waited for intermission. When the ticket collector left the door unguarded for a few seconds, Harry slipped inside and mingled with the crowd at the concession stand. At first everything went as planned. He was cool. He bought the items we wanted and took his time putting them into his pocket. But then he panicked. Not far away from him was a white kid he used to play with. The boy saw him and looked at him hard. Harry got so nervous that he didn't wait for his change. He bolted out the door and took off running. When we finally caught up with Harry, he told us what had happened. The white kid had not said anything, but just the look had been enough to make Harry take flight.

Harry wasn't the only light-skinned black person who could get around Jim Crow laws by passing for white. I knew of many light-skinned black people who got away with shopping and eating at white-only establishments because the white owner didn't know they were black. Remember how I told you that it was illegal for a black man to associate with a white woman? Here is how people got around that Jim Crowism. The white woman would ride in the backseat of a vehicle, and her black husband or boyfriend would drive the car as a chauffeur, cap and all. The local whites never sensed a thing. There were other little tricks we would play on white folks just to have a little fun. Sometimes we had to laugh to keep from crying.

CHAPTER 6

LESSONS FROM NED

My siblings and I were programmed to succeed in spite of Jim Crow. Mama and Daddy encouraged us to take advantage of every opportunity inside and outside of school to expand our knowledge.

My elementary school principal and Scoutmaster, Mr. Hall, gave me my first chance to see the world beyond Prince Edward County. He would take a small group of us on road trips whenever he and our parents could afford it—usually about once a year. He would always make us read up about a place ahead of time so that we understood the importance of what we were seeing. One of his favorite places was Petersburg, Virginia. There he would gleefully tell us how during the Civil War Ulysses S. Grant chased Robert E. Lee from that city to Appomattox.

In high school, membership on the student council and various teams, including football, track, and debate, created more opportunities to travel. We would go to competitions and conferences at other black schools in Virginia. Black businessmen would invite us to attend conferences outside the county that would expose us to different cultures. Since there were no hotels for colored people in the state at the time, our mentors found us lodging, often at black colleges. I spent so much time on the campus of Virginia State College (now known as Virginia State University) that some people thought I was a student there!

My experience on the debate team taught me to feel comfortable speaking in public. Remember how my daddy used to make us read and analyze news stories? I put that experience to work to become a skilled debater. But perhaps most important were the leadership skills I learned from being part of New Farmers of America.

New Farmers of America was the black counterpart of Future Farmers of America, which at the time was for whites only. To be a member, you had to maintain certain standards of behavior and keep your grades up. Mr. James McLendon, Dr. Calvin Anderson, and Mr. Thomas Mayfield were my high school agricultural instructors and my mentors. They all took me under their wings and helped me not only become a member but also to move into leadership positions.

Members of New Farmers learned how to evaluate and judge the performance of crops, livestock, and even farmers. Our opinions were very much respected among the community. As we liked to say back then, we had it "going on"—the New Farmers of America were "rolling." I became the organization's county and regional president, which meant I was the leader of a five-county region. For a time, I also served as state president.

One of the major projects given to our group was to raise 25 to 30 varieties of hybrid corn. We could look at the corn and tell which variety it was by the kernels. We graded each kind according to the number of bushels that were harvested from it. It just so happened that I won the contest for raising and harvesting the greatest number of bushels per acre. I did it using old reliable Ned.

The other students all pulled their plows the usual way—with a horse, a mule, or a tractor. They used to tease me because I had an ox. I didn't care because I got better results than they did. Ned walked where I wanted him to go. When I guided him with the rope so he would be in the center of a row of corn, he repeated that command for the whole acre. He was an obedient animal, and he worked well with me. Together we won that first-place award!

Our family had plowed with Ned ever since I was a little boy. We trained him just like you would a horse, so that's the way Ned responded. "Gee" meant turn right. "Yea" meant turn left. "Whoa" meant stop. "Giddy up" *(kkkkk)* meant go forward. In the beginning, it was not easy getting Ned to work. He wanted to lie around, eating. Often, Ned would stretch out like a hog being scalded when he got tired of working. We had to break him of that habit. How did my family do that? Well, it was Carrie's idea. She thought getting the dog to bark at Ned would scare him and make him get up. So, Mama and Daddy "put the dogs on Ned," and that animal got up and never attempted to lie down again when it was time to plow or do any work.

Ned worked endlessly once he was properly trained, and he served many purposes. When the time came for us to build a new house, Ned showed how strong he truly was.

We had trees in the forest on our land that had

been standing for at least 30 or 40 years—huge, beautiful trees. Daddy did not have money to pay anyone with a tractor to come over to help move the logs after the trees were cut down, so we had to make do with what we had. We took Ned and used him to snake up (move) the smaller ones. Then, Ned moved the medium-size logs. Finally, we put skids under the biggest ones to make them easier for Ned to pull. What happened when the going got tough? Well, Ned did not give up. He fell right down on his knees, stuck his front hooves in the dirt, and pulled himself forward. Once he got the logs moving, he stood back up and hauled the load. Thanks to Ned, we snaked all of the logs for our new home into place.

Ned did everything that any other animal could do, except for one thing. He did not move fast. Ned was as slow as molasses in the wintertime. When we complained about Ned, Daddy would tell us the story of the tortoise and the hare. According to the fable, the two creatures engaged in a race. The tortoise won because, unlike the hare, he was patient and kept on task. Well, Ned and I were like the tortoise. When we stuck together we eventually accomplished whatever task we took on.

CHAPTER 7

THE SKY DID NOT FALL

N one of my travels for school or even with New Farmers of America can compare with what I experienced on my first trip across the Mason-Dixon Line. My sister Martha was an officer in the United States Army Nursing Corps, stationed at Fort Dix, in New Jersey. When Carrie and I were about 16, she took us to New York City as a special treat.

I will never forget my first bus ride on that trip. I was heading to the back of the bus as colored folks had to do in the South, when Martha called out to me.

"Johnny, what are you doing?" she asked. "Why are you way back there? We aren't in the South anymore. Come sit up front with Carrie and me."

Man, oh man, I thought to myself. You mean I can actually sit up front in the section that is normally reserved for white people only? I don't have to go to the back of the bus as I do at home? As I walked back to the front of the bus to take a seat near my sisters, I realized that there were people of different colors and races scattered throughout the bus. Wow! I thought. I cannot believe this. Here we are, three colored people sitting within three rows of the front of this bus, and the sky is not falling! No one said a word or even looked at us funny. There was absolutely no trouble at all.

Why was I so surprised? Well you see, we had been programmed by certain white people in the South to believe that bad things would happen if black people and white people gathered together for any activity. As you have seen, one of the easiest ways to get in trouble was to violate the code of conduct between whites and blacks. One way we had of warning a fellow black person that he or she was in danger of stepping over the line was to say, "You don't want the sky to fall, do you?"

The sky did not fall on us during our entire vacation up North in spite of the fact that we rode beside and rubbed elbows with peoples of all races, creeds, and colors while we were in New York and New Jersey. The merchants in those states saw and recognized only one color—green. We witnessed many blacks working in key positions—operating buses, trains, and subways, being ticket agents, and even police officers—and the sky was not falling.

Nothing could compare with the fellowship I experienced sitting in the stands at Ebbets Field, in the Flatbush area of Brooklyn, New York, and watching Jackie Robinson, Roy Campanella, and the rest of the Brooklyn Dodgers play baseball. Robinson and Campanella were the first blacks to play ball for the Dodgers. We knew Roy Campanella. He held free baseball clinics on our high school athletic field during the winter months when he and his wife visited relatives in a neighboring county. He would talk to us about Jim Crow, how he was dealing with it, and how we needed to deal with it.

We went to three games at Ebbets Field. Each time there were thousands of people in the stands. The noise level created by these cheering, yelling fans was incredible. All of us were sitting elbow to elbow. None of the white people got up and moved to another seat because the three of us sat down next to them. No one called us names or insulted us.

After visiting New York City, we spent a few days at Fort Dix. Once again we saw people of all colors and creeds. The housing units were not separate, or segregated. The nurses, doctors, specialists, and technicians worked together in the hospital. Everywhere we saw people working and living together for the good of a cause, and the sky was not falling on any of them.

Of course life in the North was not without its problems and prejudices. But it was a world away from what Carrie and I were used to back home in Prince Edward County. Within this Northern culture, I saw colored, white, Hispanic, and other racial and ethnic groups all standing side-by-side and working together. They were not arguing, cussing, fussing, or causing any type of disorder or disturbance. Certain whites in the South always told us that it was impossible for blacks and whites to work together in harmony. What I witnessed on this trip fixed in my mind what Mama, Daddy, and my older brothers who had served in World War II had always told me: Those white people had been lying to us all of this time.

White fear of black people had become part of the Southern culture in which we lived. It was this fear that allowed an oligarchy—a small but powerful group of white racist bigots—to control the heartbeat of an entire region and create and maintain the Jim Crow South. What was the basis of this fear? People tend to fear the unknown, and back then white people didn't know nearly as much about black people as black people knew about them. For generations, Negroes had worked in their fields and in their homes, cooking, cleaning, and caring for their children. There was also concern that if blacks became educated, they would take away jobs and opportunities for advancement from white people. But most of all, they feared losing the purity of their race. They believed that if blacks were not kept separate from whites the result would be a mixed society. It was this fear that led to the creation of the concept of "separate but equal" and established it as the law of the land in 1896.

A couple of years after this vacation, I went back to New Jersey. This time I was with my friend Melvin Watkins. We had summer jobs working the evening shift at Woolworth's on the Boardwalk in Atlantic City. After work we would walk the "boards" with some of the other kids we worked with—Frannie and Shelby were from Philadelphia, Douglas and Robert were from some place in West Virginia, and Teresa and Jennifer were from North Carolina. We were all high school students, 17 or 18 years old. Melvin and I were black; they were white. There were many police officers patrolling the area, but not one of them told us we were breaking the law by being together in public.

No one stared at our group or moved out of the way. It was really amazing. Back home there would have been looks of dismay and disgust from angry white citizens and threats from the police.

The amazement continued as we all took seats together at a delicatessen, ordered our food, and ate it. The manager did not order any of us to move to another spot. In fact, no one paid any attention to us.

Our group represented lots of different backgrounds. Doug would always laugh and say that he belonged to the Hillbilly race. He was a little uncomfortable around Melvin and me when he first met us. He kept his distance. But as the summer wore on, his attitude changed. Once while we were working in the dishwashing room, he and Melvin bumped elbows. Doug jumped back and looked down at his skin where Melvin had touched him. Then he smiled at Melvin. "Wow, the black didn't rub off!"

Doug told us that he had been raised to believe that black people were bad news and that he should stay away from them. He also had been told that the black color would rub off. Doug now realized that the folks back home had lied to him. All I could think was, welcome to the club.

CHAPTER 8

SEPARATE BUT NEVER EQUAL

All my travels and experiences taught me that *Plessy v. Ferguson* was a hoax. It was nothing more than a way of keeping people in bondage. There was simply no way that anyone could look at the schools for blacks and whites in Prince Edward County and say they were equal. The inequalities existed throughout the history of the county's education system.

Prior to 1923, the highest level a black student could reach in Prince Edward County was sixth grade. Gradually, as a result of petitions presented by parents of black students to the Prince Edward County school board, seventh grade was added to the elementary schools. All of these grades were within a single one- or two-room wooden building that was heated with a wood or coal stove and that had no indoor toilet or running water.

More than 30 years passed between the Supreme Court's "separate but equal" ruling in 1896 and the construction of the county's first and only high school for blacks in 1927. During this same time period, six high schools for whites were built. These were located in Farmville, Worsham, Rice, Green Bay, Darlington Heights, and Prospect in what formed almost a ring around the county. Each was a brick building with indoor plumbing, central heat, up-to-date textbooks, and a library. Some had a science lab, a gymnasium, and a cafeteria. By 1947, four of these schools were converted to white elementary schools when the county decided to consolidate its high schools and send all white students to either Farmville or Worsham.

Where did colored students attend high school before 1927? Well, some students simply didn't. The more fortunate ones attended high school in another county or they left home to live in another state.

In 1927, the county finally built a high school for black students. All black children wishing to attend school beyond the seventh grade had to find a way to get to Robert Russa Moton School, in Farmville. No bus service of any kind was available to the high school until 1939. Even then, only secondhand,

Mission Elementary School for blacks

Segregated Schools in Prince Edward County in 1951

H High School for Blacks	H̄ High School for Whites
E Elementary School for Blacks	Ē Elementary School for Whites
	✳ High School for Whites before 1947

◆ other points of interest

⑮ U.S. route

㊺ ⑥⑤⑧ Virginia state route

———— primary highway

———— secondary highway

—·— county boundary

∿ river

This map is based on information provided
by Dr. Edward H. Peeples, Richmond, Virginia.
Photographs of most of these schools appear at
www.library.vcu.edu/jbc/speccoll/pec.html

states with public schools
segregated by law in 1951

Green Bay Elementary School for whites

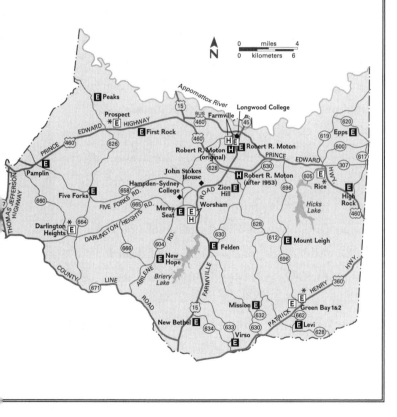

poorly maintained buses were provided for black students. By that time, my older brother Clem and my sister Martha had already graduated. Neither Howard or Leslie ever rode the bus.

The school was named for an African-American educator and lawyer who was born in 1867 in Amelia County, Virginia, which is just to the northeast of Prince Edward County. Robert Russa Moton was elected as president of the National Negro Business League in 1900, a position he held for 20 years. In 1908, Moton worked with Booker T. Washington. Born a slave, Booker T. Washington gained prominence as a spokesman for African Americans. Together, these men called on blacks and whites to work together to advance the lives of colored people by providing vocational education—schools that would provide training in a trade or skill.

The school was the first brick school built for colored children of any age in Prince Edward County. In the beginning, the first floor served as the local elementary school, while the upper floor was for the county's entire population of colored high school students. The colored students were so hungry for knowledge that they quickly filled the building. It's been told that one person commented on the number of students in the school by saying, "They are coming out of the windows!" Of course, only children who could walk to school could attend, as the county did not provide any buses for black students back then. In 1939, 12 years and numerous petitions later, the Prince Edward County school system opened a second Robert Russa Moton building. The first Robert Russa Moton school became an elementary school. That's where Carrie and I first went to school. We attended high school at the second Robert Russa Moton facility.

Both schools were located in Farmville, the county seat. County officials could point to these two brick structures as evidence that they were providing equal facilities for black students. The truth is that the new high school, built to hold 180 students, was inadequate from the start. It was a one-story building with an office, eight classrooms, and an auditorium with folding chairs rather than permanent seats. There was no gymnasium, cafeteria, or laboratory for science classes. Students used secondhand textbooks and had access to very few other resources. As the population increased, the school board refused to acknowledge the need to build another school. By the time I was a senior in 1950, there were more than 450 students.

The white school board's solution to this over-crowding was to add three wood-frame structures with tar-paper walls. Now, if you're not sure what tar paper is, it is heavy paper covered in tar that is used for waterproofing and wind proofing buildings. No brick, mortar, or wood covered the walls. Tar paper provided the only insulation.

Each classroom in these tar-paper structures was heated with a stove. As you probably know, it can get downright chilly in Virginia from time to time. Student comfort level depended on where they were seated. Those students whose desks were nearest to the potbellied stove roasted, while the students located farthest away from the stove felt cold all day. The tar-paper structures were leaky, too. Every time it rained, water dripped in. Then there were the smells. Mix the peculiar odor of tar paper with the exhaust from the school buses and fumes from the potbellied stove, and you have a pretty obnoxious odor that students had to endure day in and day out. It was almost as though the white power structure forgot that the students had the use of their five senses. Can you imagine trying to learn under these awful conditions?

We were the laughingstock of the area. People

passing through would ask, "Who owns the chicken farm?" When they found out the buildings were part of a school, some would take pictures to show the people back home how backward we were. I often thought how ironic life is. Those cows that I used to milk before school every morning lived in a more secure structure than the shacks we attended classes in. So much for being separate but equal.

The principal of our high school, Mr. M. Boyd Jones, had a running battle with the school superintendent, Mr. McIlwaine. Mr. Jones would ask, "When are you going to do something about these tar-paper structures? They're leaking. They are inadequately insulated. There are no toilet facilities in them. We have an enrollment of more than 450 students in a school that was set up for 180 students."

The Prince Edward County school board always had the same answer: "Oh, we're working on it. We can't find the land for a new facility." When John Lancaster, who was the county farm agent for the colored people, and Reverend L. Francis Griffin, one of the chief spiritual leaders of colored people in Prince Edward County, found some land, the white school board officials found an excuse for not purchasing it.

The colored people in Prince Edward County were not blind. It was easy to see that schools for blacks in our county were not equal to those for white children. Students like myself who had traveled to participate in interscholastic events knew that our schools were not even equal to schools for blacks in other counties in Virginia.

My brother Clem, who had graduated from Hampton Institute (now Hampton University), in Virginia, was a teacher and principal at New Hope, one of the county's elementary schools, after he got out of the Army. He often spoke to the superintendent about the inequities and requested funds to purchase additional resources for his students, but his pleas fell on deaf ears.

Other veterans told how they had been accepted and treated better in Europe than in their own country and how difficult it was to return home to Virginia and be treated as second-class citizens.

Sometimes I think being older—I was 19 during my senior year—gave me an advantage in evaluating our situation at Robert Russa Moton High School. I understood the indignities we were made to face daily as we tried to learn in those tar-paper shacks. But I soon found out that I was not alone. There were others who realized that the kettle had grown too hot to hold everything inside. The top was about to blow off. We could no longer endure the wretched conditions at Robert Russa Moton High School. We had to find a way to persuade our local school board to build us a new school.

We decided to call a strike!

CHAPTER 9

OUR MANHATTAN PROJECT

The strike was the brainchild of Barbara Johns. She had read about how some white students at a girls' school up North had gone on strike to get better dining room facilities. It had worked for them, so she was determined to make it work for us.

Barbara came to Carrie and me in October 1950, just as our senior year was getting under way. Who was she, and why did she seek us out? As a 16-year-old sophomore, she understood that she would need the support of school leaders if her plan were to succeed. I was president of the senior class. She also knew that Carrie and I came from a family that was respected by blacks and whites alike in Prince Edward County. She had heard that we had traveled outside of the South and, as a result, that we were well aware of how poorly our school measured up against not only white schools but also other black schools outside the county. She believed that my experiences with New Farmers of America and the debate team would be critical assets to accomplishing her goal.

She wanted the students of Robert Russa Moton High School to strike—to walk out and refuse to attend classes—until a new school building was under construction. She said that the parents' plan to work through the Moton P.T.A. to put pressure on the school board to make changes wasn't working. She had an idea that would broadcast Prince Edward County all over the world.

I had heard others speak about leading a revolt against the system. I had ignored them because I did not feel that their plans were well thought out. I also did not trust them. But Barbara Johns was different. There was something very special and genuine about her that is really hard to put into words. There was something unique about her demeanor that commanded my respect. It made me not only trust her, but also have faith in her ability to take us to this Promised Land—a new school building. She was a very quiet person and very much a lady. But once Barbara Johns homed in on an idea, she was like a Sidewinder missile locked on its target. She was tenacious. Once she decided that we needed to strike, she kept handing me notes and following me around. She was persistent, and she was convincing. Finally, I agreed to meet with her on the cinder block bleachers at our school's athletic field.

I had heard of strikes, boycotts, and things like that, so these concepts were not new to me. But I wasn't convinced that they would work for us. Barbara changed my mind. Once she had corralled me and was looking me straight in the eye, I knew that if anyone could pull this off, she could. I'll never forget her words. She said, "I'll die for the cause." I knew she was right, and I knew I could not live with myself if I did not support her plan. We started planning the strike right there and then. We knew it was not going to be easy, but we believed we could pull it off.

We called our secret plan the "Manhattan Project," adopting the code name given to the top secret effort developed by the United States and some of its allies during World War II to produce the first nuclear weapons. I had learned about the success of that project from my father. Knowing we had to maintain strict secrecy in our planning, we thought "Manhattan Project" fit our endeavor. As I saw it, the two projects were similar. There was going to be quite an explosion if the strike went as planned.

Selecting the right people to help us carry out our plan would be key to its success. Character and leadership skills were the most important criteria. People wouldn't follow us if they didn't respect us. Candidates also had to be trustworthy. We had to be sure that they would not reveal anything about the strike to anyone outside the planning committee. Finally, we had to have representatives from different areas of the county—students who understood how people in their regions thought, how they would react, and who could solve problems that might arise in a particular locality. We had to pass over some of the people who were especially outspoken and who we thought would have made strong leaders in the coalition because we knew their parents would stop their participation.

Eventually, 20 students formed the core strike force. Each person was a leader in a different way and brought particular strengths to our Manhattan Project. Who were some of these warriors? One was Loreda Branch, one of my favorite classmates.

Loreda was very quiet, but when it became necessary, she could hold her own. She was a deep thinker and extremely levelheaded about our plan to strike against the system. You knew where you stood with Loreda. While she was a lovely and gentle person, she always remained strong.

Another key committee member was Irene Taylor, an officer on the student council who represented the Leigh Mountain District. It was extremely critical to have a leader from Leigh District because it was a farming area, and agriculture was key to the county's economy. People's livelihoods there depended on being able to buy supplies and sell their crops, things that were controlled by the white power structure. Without a leader from this district, it would have been easy for our opponents to intimidate students there into returning to school before the strike achieved its goal. Irene had the charm and quiet demeanor to keep everyone focused. She won the hearts and minds of a lot of people who probably would have rebelled against us. Thanks to her, people in the Leigh District proved to be some of our strongest supporters.

Throughout our project, secrecy was the top priority. I even had my own code names for the committee members. Barbara Johns was General

Groves, named for General Leslie R. Groves, who directed the original Manhattan Project. I named myself and each of the 18 other committee members J. Robert Oppenheimer, after its scientific director. I imagined that all of our supporters were based at Oak Ridge, Tennessee, or Los Alamos, New Mexico. I code named Robert Russa Moton High School "Trinity," after the site in New Mexico where the first atomic bomb was tested. The leaders of the original Manhattan Project did their planning with discretion, thoroughness, and dispatch. We did, too. Barbara Johns held her first formal meeting with the committee at the high school football field—on the same cinder block bleachers where she and I had met. Even though we were only high school students, we planned this thing to a gnat's eyebrow.

We promised each other not to reveal our activities to any friend or relative—not even brothers and sisters—during the planning phase. Our fear was that they might accidentally say something to someone that would expose us. We were concerned about protecting not only our plan but also the principal and teachers at the school. We knew that if the school board got wind of what we were up to they would blame the principal and teachers for not stopping us.

They could all lose their jobs, and we did not want that on our consciences. They had taught us to be leaders—to be the best we could be at all times. We admired and respected them and didn't want to cause them trouble. They along with our parents had instilled in us a positive attitude. We took pride in knowing that we were going to make something of ourselves no matter what.

That's why it came as quite a shock when we learned that "Spike" had gotten wind of our plan. Spike was our code name for Mr. W. Boyd Jones, our principal. Who told Spike? What did he know? If he knew, who else did? Was our Manhattan Project in jeopardy? These were some of the questions that raced through the minds of the strike committee as we made our final plans. We had taken pride in how careful we were being. Now Spike might disrupt everything. We went into action immediately. We fed the suspected informer bits and pieces of misinformation just as all good spies would do. It worked. The principal decided the rumors were unfounded.

You might wonder how we learned to do all this? Well, we were products of our own era. We had just lived through World War II. The media was filled with stories about spies and counterspies. And we had heard countless war stories from combat veterans—some about military espionage. We used what we had learned in our planning. We had to do this in order to accomplish our mission. And it worked. We encountered very few troublemakers.

The Manhattan Project members met for the last time at my family's farm in Kingsville on April 22, 1951, the day before the strike. Some of the project members wondered if we would be put in jail if we went through with our plan to strike. We decided to ask my brother Leslie if he thought that was a possibility. He asked us how many students attended Robert Russa Moton High School. We said that 450 students were currently enrolled. Next, Leslie asked us how big the Farmville jail was. We immediately understood why we did not need to be concerned about spending any time there. The jail was too small to fit that many people. At the time, Leslie had no idea that we were actually planning a strike. He probably thought we needed the information for some kind of school project. We did, but not for the kind of project he imagined!

Reassured, we made our specific decisions. We checked the weather report. We wanted to be certain that the weather was going to be good the next day.

Next, we reviewed everyone's responsibilities to make sure that each person understood what he or she was supposed to do.

At last, we were ready. There was no turning back. Only by moving ahead did we have any hope of achieving a more equal school system for the black people of Prince Edward County. It had taken six months of courage, endurance, and trust to make our Manhattan Project ready for action.

"D-Day" was April 23, 1951.

CHAPTER 10

THERE'S A RIOT AT THE SCHOOL

The first order of business for the strike committee on Monday morning, April 23, 1951, was to get our principal, Mr. Jones, to leave the campus. Specific students were selected to plant themselves at strategic locations in Farmville. From those vantage points, they made telephone calls to Mr. Jones. Pretending to be adults, they complained that some of his students were downtown creating problems in key public places. Mr. Jones was a strict disciplinarian who never let his students do anything wrong. Just as we knew he would, Mr. Jones left the campus in a huff to check things out.

As soon as we saw him leave, we sent a note around to each classroom telling everyone to go to the auditorium for an emergency meeting. Barbara

Johns wrote those notes and scribbled her initials, B.J., at the bottom. Everyone assumed "B.J." stood for Boyd Jones. There was no reason to think otherwise. It was a normal occurrence for our principal to call an emergency meeting if anything went wrong, even if it was only about someone littering in the school-yard. He was a gung-ho stickler for following rules.

By the time all the students arrived in the audi-torium, the members of the strike committee were sitting on stage behind a drawn curtain. When the curtain opened, I stood up and got the students to quiet down. We opened the assembly with the Pledge of Allegiance. Then we said the Lord's Prayer and sang a song. I don't remember what song it was.

After the singing, a committee member asked all the teachers to leave. We knew that if they stayed they could be fired for supporting us, and we didn't want that to happen. They all left except one teacher. He ended up going but not until he was assisted by a couple of nice-size football players. They put him in a class-room and stood guard to make certain he would stay put. We had heard that this teacher was a stooge of the power structure. We wanted to be sure that he couldn't alert them. Two of the other teachers sneaked back into the auditorium. We saw them in

This photograph captures one of the proudest moments in my life—the night that I was awarded the Charles Hamilton Houston, Sr., Pioneer for Justice Award at a ceremony in Constitution Hall commemorating the 50th anniversary of Brown v. Board of Education. *Dr. Charles Hamilton Houston, Sr., who died before this landmark decision was made, became known as "the man who killed Jim Crow" for his tireless efforts to end legalized segregation*

Scouting taught me survival skills—how to deal with people and situations—skills that I use every day of my life. Here I am in my full uniform, standing at attention in our front yard.

We depended on our ox Ned to help us with all kinds of chores on our farm. Here, Daddy and Ned work together to remove snow, using a homemade plow.

This photograph of the standing-room-only crowd at the First Baptist Church in Farmville the night we signed the petition for a nonsegregated high school was published in the **Richmond Afro-American** *newspaper.*

This photograph shows (left to right) Admore Joyner, me, Thelma Allen, and Rome Matthews in front of the cross that was burned at our school.

The top photograph shows one of the tar-paper structures that served as extra classrooms at Robert Russa Moton High School. Below is the new, state-of-the-art Robert Russa Moton High School that opened in 1953. It, along with all other public schools in the county, was closed for five years (1959–1964) during the era of Massive Resistance. Now called Prince Edward County High School, it is fully integrated.

there, but we knew that they wouldn't create a ruckus. They were harmless.

Barbara Johns addressed the student body first. That's when everyone learned why we had called the assembly. She spoke about the inequalities we were forced to face each day. She explained that nothing would change unless we joined together and demanded a new school facility. Everyone listened intently.

We were packed in that room like sardines in a can. It was warm. It was stuffy. But soon everyone was at a fever pitch. Even the shy students caught the spirit as we began singing pep songs. When I saw those quiet, doubting, innocent-acting students shouting, "Two bits—four bits—six bits—a dollar—all for this strike stand up and holler," I knew that we were on a roll. We had gotten the principal and almost all the teachers to leave, and we had won over the pessimists and the quiet ones to our side. I felt nothing could stop our strike now.

Man, you talk about rocking. No one was seated. It was like a heavy thunderstorm in full force. I thought to myself, all we need now is for lightning to strike. And lightning did strike. It came in the form of my mother. Right in the middle of one of my cheers, I happened to glance at the entrance door.

There stood Mrs. Alice Maria Spraggs Stokes, my mama, with her girlfriend Mrs. Daisy Anderson. I froze. How in the world did she find out about what was going on? Who told her? Was she going to make us call the whole thing off? Most of the students knew her. So did most of the people in the community—the teachers, preachers, merchants, and others. They all respected her. She appeared calm and composed, but I could see that she was evaluating the entire situation. She took it all in. Blocking out the noise and excitement engulfing her, she looked directly at me.

Recovered from my frozen state, I gathered myself, went down the stage steps, and approached her.

"Mama," I said.

She looked me dead in the eyes and asked, "Son are you all all right?"

"Yes, Mama," I answered.

She repeated, "No, I mean, are you **all** all right?"

Again I answered, "Yes, Mama."

She turned and very calmly said, "OK, Daisy, let's go!" She and her friend turned and walked out. WOW! What a relief.

Later, I found out that one of the girls had left the campus and had run up Route 15 screaming that there was a riot at the high school—the entire student body was upset and was meeting in the auditorium. Of course there never was a riot. The whole thing was very peaceful, but Mama couldn't have known that then. When she heard the girl, she must have thought, "Lord, my children are down there."

After Mama left the room, I knew all systems were go. I knew that I would have Daddy's support, too. If Mama had said to me, "Boy, you are calling this thing off," I would not be writing this book today. I would have said to the students, "Ladies and gentlemen, head back to your classes. The strike is off." In fact, if any member of the strike committee had backed out at this time, the strike would have fallen apart, and the entire cause would have been lost. The movement had not yet gained any momentum. We needed all hands on deck to get this ship out of port!

Meanwhile, people in town continued to hear that there was an uprising at the colored high school. News traveled like wildfire in Farmville. As parents and others hurried down to the school to check out the rioting and to be certain all of the students were safe, they entered the auditorium. Instead of finding bedlam, they found an orderly group of student leaders having an assembly. Yet, something strange seemed to be going on. There was no principal, and no teachers were in sight except for the two who were peeping around the corner. None of the parents took their children home. They ended up leaving the school, while the kids remained.

When our principal returned from his wild goose chase, he had a puzzled look on his face. I think that he was upset by what greeted him even though there was no real disturbance. What he saw was not a riot but a very orderly strike led by his students. We had been taught to respect authority. We knew that the only path to accomplishing our goal of gaining a new school had to be a peaceful one.

Outside the building, some of the students were carrying picket signs that we had made up ahead of time. The messages urged the building of a new school and the destruction of the tar-paper structures. There was talk of continuing the picketing until the school board set a date for construction of a new school to begin.

The picketing didn't last long. Word came from the superintendent's office that if we weren't going to attend classes, we had to get off school property. If we didn't, we would be arrested for trespassing. That day students went home by their usual means of transportation. Although some parents when they found out about the strike thought we should not pursue it, most of them backed it. They were well aware of the conditions at the school and knew that their own efforts to bring change had met with one broken promise after another.

As leaders of the strike, we spoke that day with our principal and our parents, informing all of them that we were dissatisfied. We told them that we were not going back to class until something was done. We were striking for a new school. That was it. We also tried to meet with Superintendent McIlwaine, but he refused to see us.

While we were trying to figure out a way to talk to the school board, Mr. John Lancaster and Reverend L. Francis Griffin arrived at the school. Mr. Lancaster was the president of our P.T.A. He and his committee had gone head to head with the school board in an attempt to get a new school and other things for colored students and teachers but had been turned down repeatedly. He would become one of our key mentors during the strike. He was fired up all of the time, and we fed off of his energy.

Reverend Griffin, who was pastor of the First Baptist Church in Farmville, told us that we could use his church as a meeting place. He was president of the local chapter of the NAACP (the National Association for the Advancement of Colored People), and he advised us to contact lawyers in the NAACP's Richmond office for legal help with our strike. Founded in 1909, the NAACP is our country's oldest civil rights group.

Carrie and Barbara Johns wasted no time in calling the Richmond office. The lawyers were out of town dealing with another case, so the representative they spoke with suggested that they write a letter explaining the situation. Together, Barbara and Carrie drafted a letter, telling them about the strike and asking them to come to Farmville on Wednesday, April 25. They even told them that we would provide a place for them to stay if they needed overnight accommodations (remember at this time there were no hotels for black people in Prince Edward County). Carrie typed it up, and then one of the committee members took it directly to the post office. We felt we couldn't trust any outsider, not even the postman.

Day one of the strike had ended.

CHAPTER 11

TAKING CARE OF BUSINESS

I n the following days, our committee was kept busy. We had a series of meetings with people, both white and black, in positions of power, and we had to make sure the Moton students and their parents stood firm.

The first order of business was to make sure that students who were absent on the day of the strike did not go to school the next day. We were also concerned that some of the parents of the kids who had been at school and who had agreed to stay out on strike might make their kids get on the buses. If this had happened and just one of these kids had gone into the school building, the strike would have ended. Therefore, for the first few days after the strike began, committee members maintained a checkpoint at a location just outside the high school grounds. Our job was to intercept the buses, let the students get off, and then get them home safely in vehicles on loan to us from local black businessmen. They had agreed to let us use their vehicles so long as we returned each one with a full tank of gas. We paid for the gas out of our own pockets.

Only eight students arrived at school the day after the strike. Because they had been absent the day before, they had no idea what had gone on at school. Their families didn't have telephones, and even if they had a radio, it wouldn't have mattered. There was no news coverage about the strike until several days later. Catherine Coles and Carrie talked to the students, explained what was going on, and told them why they had to go home. Not one of them gave us any trouble. They just got in the cars and let us take them home.

One of the students I drove home was a girl named Celeste. She warned me that her father might be upset, more because a boy was bringing her home than because of the strike. (Her father had warned her never to get into a car alone with a boy.) She wanted to know all about why we called the strike. To help her understand what we hoped to gain, I asked her about the elementary school she attended before coming to Moton. Asking her that question was like letting all the water out of the Hoover Dam. Tears welled up in her eyes as she talked. Her school had been one of those typical black rural schools that had been neglected by the power structure for years. It was a small wooden building on stilts, located on a church ground. (The school board often did this to save money.) Animals often made their homes under the building. Many times there was no heat because there was no firewood for the stove. The only source for drinking water was an open-top well. Students had to all drink out of the same cup or dipper that hung on the side of the well.

She smiled slightly when she confessed how one day she and a friend had done a dangerous thing: They had sneaked into a white school in the Green Bay area after hours. Even though she could see from the outside that the school was in much better shape than hers, she was still surprised by what she saw inside. There were many more classrooms than she had imagined, and not a single one had a wood stove. Instead, she discovered that there was a huge boiler system that supplied the entire building with heat. There was more than one toilet, and none of them smelled. She drank water from fountains inside the school and saw book after book after book on the shelves in the library. She said that going back to her one-room school after seeing the white students' school made her sick to her stomach. "After all," she said, "I am a human being, too."

When we arrived at Celeste's house, her father was working a team of mules. We had to wait for him to make his rounds back to the house. I introduced myself and explained why I had brought his daughter home. I also told him some of the things Celeste had told me about her school and the Green Bay school. He became very animated. He knew that conditions at Celeste's elementary school hadn't changed since he'd been a student there. He also knew that racial inequalities weren't limited to the schools. He said he was experiencing it in the sale of his crops. His voice got louder as he said that it was past time to do something to change things. He wanted to know how he could help. I promised to keep him posted about parent support meetings he could attend, then he shook my hand and said good-bye. He had work to do, and so did I, back in Farmville.

As Celeste's dad made his way back across the field to his team of mules, he yelled back, "You are Mrs. Alice Stokes's son, aren't you, boy?" When I told him I was, he said, "I know your mama and daddy quite well. Decent people. Give them my regards, you hear. And by the way, John, thanks for getting Celeste home safely."

His words made me feel proud.

That Tuesday afternoon, 19 members of the strike committee marched into a meeting with Mr. McIlwaine in the county courthouse. We carried ourselves with dignity and poise. We were focused and determined. Mr. McIlwaine had told us to meet him in the courtroom rather than his office. When we arrived, he was sitting in the judge's chair on a raised stand. He motioned for us to sit down in the chairs below him. It was obvious that he was trying to intimidate us, but it didn't work. We had done our homework and wasted no time telling him what we wanted: a date for when construction would begin on the new high school for blacks. The school had been part of the county's school improvement plan for years, but to date no ground had been broken for it. We wanted to know what the holdup was.

Mr. McIlwaine said that the decision regarding the building of a new school was up to the school board. He explained that funds had been put away for a new school, but the amount was only one-third of what the school would actually cost. The superintendent complained that it was hard trying to get something without having enough money. He said that the amount of taxes black people paid was only about 10 percent of all taxes collected in Prince Edward County. He said that our strike would cost the county school system $100 for every day we stayed out of school. In other words, we were hurting ourselves by striking, since it would take money from the fund to build the new school.

He told us that representatives had been sent to our school and had concluded that the facilities were good. As for the tar-paper buildings, they were only temporary structures. He had the nerve to tell us that every piece of furniture in Moton was just as nice as in any other school in Prince Edward County. He also claimed that the equipment in the agricultural building at Moton was the most up-to-date in the county.

We knew that all of this was a lie. If he had ever set foot in our school (which we knew he hadn't), he would realize how absurd his words were. If he had just once stepped into one of the tar-paper shacks, he would not only have seen the inequalities between our high school and the white high school in Farmville, he would have heard them, felt them, tasted them, and smelled them. He would have realized that these structures were not fit even for animals.

Our committee had gathered information that substantiated what we already knew about the Prince

Edward County school system: that the schools for colored students were not equal to any of those for white children. The property value of the white schools was estimated to be around $1.2 million dollars. In contrast, the colored schools were valued at around $327,000 dollars! Records show that the amount of money spent by the county on each white student at the time was $817 compared with only $194 spent on each black student.

Mr. McIlwaine told us that people who had lived in Prince Edward County over the past 20 years were amazed at what had been done by the school board. He said, "The only money that has been spent since 1937 has been spent for Negro schools." He went on to say that the amount of money needed to build a new school for us would be more than most schools had cost. For this reason, the board would have to get the citizens to vote for a new facility. He doubted there would be support for this. His advice to us was that we should "take things as they come instead of by force." Force would lead to "hatred among the people."

As we ended the meeting, Mr. McIlwaine said he was a Christian and that he would pray for the school system. He said he couldn't demand that the school board give us a new school, but he would talk with the school board members at their next meeting. When we learned that this would not be for another two weeks, we asked him if he would contact Mr. M. R. Large, chairman of the Prince Edward County school board, and request that he call an emergency meeting of the board. Mr. McIlwaine refused.

Throughout the meeting, Mr. McIlwaine never once looked any of us directly in the eye. Mama and Daddy always told us that a person who couldn't look you in the eye was not to be trusted. That certainly was true not only of Mr. McIlwaine but also of the entire membership of the school board. When we walked out of that meeting, we knew that we were no closer to getting an answer about when we would get a new school than our parents had been with their petitions to the school board through the P.T.A. We also knew that the white power structure was stalling and that nothing was going to change under the current system. Further attempts to try to meet to talk about the issue would be a waste of time. We didn't know how to break through this logjam. Then we got a call from Reverend Griffin.

CHAPTER 12

DON'T GIVE UP

Reverend Griffin told us to get ready to meet with the NAACP lawyers. Oliver W. Hill and Spottswood W. Robinson, III, were coming to Farmville. They had gotten the letter that Carrie and Barbara had sent and wanted to talk to us.

On Wednesday, April 25, we went down to the First Baptist Church. We weren't alone. A few other students, our parents, and some other mentors came along for a show of support, but only the committee members met with the lawyers from Richmond. They told us that they were headed to another meeting in Blacksburg, but they had detoured several miles out of their way to come to Farmville. They wanted to meet the students who were leading a school strike.

Dr. Thomas Henderson was also with them. I had seen all three of these men before, but the one I felt closest to was Dr. Henderson. He often was the keynote speaker for our group at organizational meetings of New Farmers of America. I knew that he worked closely with the NAACP.

Mr. Hill and Mr. Robinson tested us during their visit; they tested our courage and our resolve. Mr. Robinson said that the NAACP did not advise students to strike, but he understood the reasons that drove us to take this action and felt they were justified. Even so, the NAACP could not help us in our demand for a school equal to the white high school. He explained that the NAACP was no longer interested in separate but equal. It was working for nonsegregation (what we call integration today) in the South. The new policy of the NAACP was to only get involved in cases that sought to overthrow separate facilities for blacks and whites. In fact, the reason that they were on their way to Blacksburg was that the NAACP was trying to win a case in Pulaski County that would allow Negro students to attend a white school. At the time Pulaski County had no black school for these students to attend, so they had to travel to another county to get an education. He told us that the NAACP would be able to back us 100 percent if we asked the Prince Edward County school authorities for a nonsegregated school rather than a new facility for colored students. In other words, we needed to ask for a facility where whites and Negroes could attend school together.

Mr. Robinson made it clear to us that he could not guarantee us any help if we chose to stick to our goal of a separate but equal school. He did promise that he and the other lawyers would discuss our case and get back to us. Meanwhile, the lawyers suggested that our parents keep us home until we heard back from the NAACP. The three men complimented us on our spunk in standing up to the white authorities and told us not to give up hope. Mr. Hill later would recall, "We found them [the Moton students] so well organized that we didn't have the heart to break their spirit."

After the meeting, the strike leaders felt a little let down and somewhat discouraged. The NAACP wanted us to change our goals, and we weren't sure that was the way to go. In spite of this, we were determined not to go back to school so long as things stayed the way they were. We agreed to stay out on strike even if the great NAACP could not help us. We had faith that somebody would come to our aid.

We felt that when 450 kids walked out of school the action ought to get somebody's attention.

Before we had time to really think about our next step, we received some hopeful news. Apparently our determination had impressed the gentlemen from the NAACP. Lester A. Banks, Executive Secretary of the Virginia Chapter of the NAACP, was going to speak to the students and parents of Robert Russa Moton High School at the P.T.A. meeting on the evening of April 26.

More than 950 people turned out to hear the fiery executive secretary speak. We opened the session by singing a hymn, "Nearer, My God, to Thee." Prayer was offered. Reverend Griffin spoke on the need for cooperation among the community and told our parents that they needed to stand by us in our demands. Then, Barbara Johns, our selected spokesperson for the Manhattan Project committee, stood up. She commanded the crowd's attention as she discussed the concerns the Robert Russa Moton High School students had about the lack of facilities and resources at our high school and described the miserable conditions of the tar-paper shacks that were used as classrooms. She told the parents how our meeting with Mr. McIlwaine had produced no results, only the promise of more delays. She also told them that if the students wanted the support of the NAACP, we would have to go beyond the concept of separate but equal. We would have to fight for a nonsegregated school. She ended by pleading with the parents to back the students in their stand against the white power structure.

Barbara was announcing for the first time what our committee had spent several hours thrashing around about. We knew that before Mr. Banks spoke at the school, we had to decide what we were going to do. We were afraid of nonsegregation, not just because of how the white power structure would retaliate but because we knew integration would dismantle our education system. We were very proud of our teachers. They were the ones who had taught us how to be leaders. They were our motivators and our role models. We knew we would lose them and these benefits when there were no longer separate schools for blacks and whites. When the strike committee finally voted, nonsegregation won by only one vote! That's how close it was. That's how close we came to not making history. But once the decision was made, we were all united behind it.

After Barbara sat down, Mr. Banks delivered a very powerful speech. He began by telling the people that since its founding 42 years before, the NAACP had been working to prepare our people "for the progress and leadership, which are due us." As recorded by my sister, Lester Banks said, "We as Negroes should not be satisfied with what we have been given." He went on to say, "We are Americans and should enjoy all the rights, privileges, and amenities as anyone else."

Then he came to the critical part. He said, "There is no such thing as separate but equal. If it is separate and equal today, it will be unequal tomorrow. Equality is a little deeper than that." According to him, the people of Prince Edward County and Farmville would hinder the Negro for years to come if they backed down on the proposition of nonsegregated schools.

When he finished, the parents were given a chance to share their opinions. People realized that in supporting nonsegregation they would be going against the Jim Crow power system. They would be overturning a way of life with roots dating back almost 350 years. There was real fear that supporting nonsegregation would rob them of their ability to make a living or would encourage Klan violence. Some voiced concerns similar to those we had discussed in our committee meeting earlier in the day. I remember one father stood up and said the parents should have been informed that the students were going to go on strike before they actually took that action. Lester Banks responded by saying, "You are saying that your child, or your children, or these children should have informed you. But the reason they did not inform you was because if they had informed you, we wouldn't be here today. There never would have been a strike."

In the end, our parents understood that we could not go to court to get an equal facility, because even if we built a school brick by brick, it would never be equal to the white schools. Some way or another the white power structure would find a way to give more to the whites than to the people of our race. We would have to do what the NAACP lawyers said. We would have to file for nonsegregation. And that is exactly what they voted for.

I was very proud of my people, proud of the black community. Even though the idea of standing up to the white power structure caused a lot of fear and uncertainty, we had not broken ranks. We had taken a stand for future generations.

CHAPTER 13

UNCHARTED WATERS

In the days following the vote, the strike committee was kept busy meeting with lawyers, our mentors and parents, and others in the black community. The lawyers were drawing up a petition for nonsegregation that would form the basis for our lawsuit against Prince Edward County. On May 3rd there would be a meeting in the First Baptist Church to sign the petition. We realized that there was a big difference between raising your hand in a closed meeting to vote for something and signing your name on a piece of paper. We had one week to talk to people and make sure we didn't lose their support.

We knew that we were in uncharted waters. We were attempting to do what no one else had tried to do before. We likened ourselves to the Biblical character Abraham. When God told him to leave his home and go to Canaan, he had no more idea where he was heading than the man in the moon. He went forth on faith alone and so did we. I had known that everything would be all right that day Alice Maria Spraggs Stokes supported us in the auditorium with her silence. Furthermore, she had prayed for Carrie and me, and when she ended her prayer, she said the angels would watch over us. I had known then that I could go through this entire voyage without fear of being harmed so long as I stayed humble and focused.

On April 27 the first article about our strike appeared on the front page of the *Farmville Herald.* The headline for the story read, "Moton Students' Claims Unjustified Board Feels Now." In the newspaper report, Mr. McIlwaine stated that the action of the students was seen as a breach of discipline. The school board noted that the timing of the strike was poor, because negotiations were being made for a site for the proposed new high school facility. When the story mentioned the students' concern over the tar-paper shacks, the reported response from the school board was that the structures had been put up temporarily in view of the construction of a new school facility in the near future. We knew that this was just an attempt to convince white residents that the school board was living up to its responsibilities under the existing separate but equal law. The white community had no idea that we had changed our goal to nonsegregation.

A couple of days later, our principal, under orders from the school board, wrote a letter to the parents of all Moton students saying that the superintendent had authorized him to request all students to return to school. If they failed to do so, there would be "grave consequences which must be suffered by those who persist in violating the compulsory attendance laws" and the students and their parents would be "subject to punishment upon the recommendation of the division superintendent." The letter was signed by Mr. Jones and all the teachers at the school.

Reverend Griffin and Mr. John Lancaster were quick to counter with their own letter to the parents. In it they indicated their support for our strike and the fight for nonsegregation and told the parents to ignore Mr. Jones's letter and keep their children home. Our committee took copies of this letter and went door to door until we had reached every household. Thanks to this swift action, parents listened to our leaders and kept their sons and daughters home.

We understood that our principal was doing what

he had to do to keep his job. The school board also tried to make Mr. Jones feel he was responsible for the student strike. The board and the superintendent looked upon him as a nondisciplinarian. They thought he should be able to make his students return to school. But the truth was there was nothing he could do about the strike. No one could have made a group of 450 kids do anything they didn't agree to do.

Our committee had several private meetings during the week after the vote for nonsegregation. One of them was at the Beulah African Methodist Episcopal (A.M.E.) Church. John Lancaster, our fiery P.T.A. president, spoke some very inspirational words to us there. He told us, "We have been trying to get the people in charge of the school system to treat us in a fair and respectful manner ever since my own daddy was the president of our P.T.A. These people have not been fair to us, and they have never respected us; they have lied to us; they have actually cheated us; they have robbed us of our educational rights. Boys and girls, you have done a wonderful job. You have done a brave thing. We are not going to let you down. We are very proud of you, and we are going to support you. There is a saying by us farmers, 'You cannot scald the hogs until the water is right.' Y'all have the water just right, so let us go forth and scald the hogs. Let us stand together and fight for our rights. You children are our future. You children are good for us. Keep on keeping on."

A couple of reporters from the *Farmville Herald* tried to get into that meeting. Of course we refused to allow them in. The upshot was an article that appeared on May 1 in the newspaper. In it the reporters expressed their shock that a group of young black students would have the nerve to shut the door in the face of white journalists. Where had they learned their manners? What were they trying to hide?

The article stirred up a lot of angry feelings. Some people even started calling us communists! In other words, they were accusing us of being un-American. We couldn't believe it. Many of my classmates and I had draft cards, which meant that we could be called up at any time to serve our country and protect these very people who were calling us communists. Yet we knew that some white boys our age managed to avoid having to register for Army service. I wondered who the real communists were!

The reaction of the white community to our strike was interesting. We heard through the grapevine that some white students from Farmville High School wanted to join us, but their parents wouldn't allow it. In fact we learned that many whites had sympathy for our cause but were afraid to support us openly because they feared they might be the target of some sort of retaliation by the white power structure. There were also a few like Jack Jeffers and his family who were convinced that separate but equal served only to create more inequality between the races. Then there were others who looked on us as though we were a school of piranhas waiting to devour them on sight. Others just seemed to wish that we would disappear.

Interestingly enough, police officers and other officials treated us very fairly. Sometimes when our committee had to cross the street and there was heavy traffic, the police would stop traffic so we could get to the other side. We suspected that they weren't doing this because they sympathized with our cause. Rather, they wanted to be sure no one could accuse them of not treating the black population fairly.

No matter what came our way, we knew that we had a job to do. We had to make people aware of the gross inequities between the blacks and whites of this community. Only by getting them to see the real situation rather than accepting as fact what they read in the paper or heard from the white power structure could we achieve lasting change.

CHAPTER 14

A SKITTISH NIGHT

The meeting to sign the petition that would authorize the NAACP to file a lawsuit for nonsegregation on our behalf took place at the First Baptist Church on May 3. As we approached downtown Farmville, we had to go through a sort of checkpoint at the edge of town. I later learned that these checkpoints were on every road leading into Farmville. Virginia state troopers were directing traffic, too. I was a little surprised because we had not publicized the meeting. But I should have realized the white authorities would know about it. They had their informers—stooges, as we called them. Some of these were white people, like those newspaper reporters I mentioned earlier. Others were some of my own people who didn't approve of what we were doing. They were more interested in saving their own skins than in thinking about the long-term benefits to future generations of black people. At any rate, the colored community had come out in force for the meeting. They were as thick as ticks on a dog! In addition to Moton parents and students, there were others who recognized the importance of what we were trying to do and came to show their support.

The strike committee was scheduled to have a pre-meeting conference with the lawyers and our mentors. To get to the basement door of the church, we had to squeeze sideways through the crowd. People were slapping us on our backs, giving us high fives, shaking our hands, and shouting words of encouragement. During our meeting in the church basement, we determined who would say what and who would sit in the pulpit at the front of the church with the lawyers and other dignitaries. Reverend Griffin warned us that no one except the lawyers should talk to the media if any were present. He also warned us that spies were likely to be in the audience. He did not have to name them because we knew exactly who he meant. Last, but not least, he told us to stay cool.

I was selected to be one of the student strike

leaders to sit in the pulpit. Man, what an honor! I
felt like a big wheel in a Georgia cotton field. I tried
to be cool as we climbed the back steps leading to the
area where the pulpit was, but it was tough. My heart
was pounding. I could hear a loud buzzing, but I was
not prepared for what I saw when we sat down.

This was the largest black church within 60
miles, and I knew it could hold at least 500 people.
It was packed, and more people were milling around
outside. Ushers had set up folding chairs in the
aisles. They were all occupied, and people were lined
up against the walls. I had never before seen that
many people in this church. I recognized many of
the folks from my work with New Farmers of
America. Some in the audience were farmers who
seldom came out at night except for an emergency.
They must have considered this an emergency.
Celeste was there, too. Her father had been one of
those who spoke to me as we were going into our
pre-meeting. He had given me one of his huge bear-
paw handshakes.

Reverend Griffin had challenged us to notify
every black person in Prince Edward County about
this emergency meeting for colored folks. Obviously
we had done our job. We had had help from the

Reverend, Mr. Lancaster, and other supporters who worked long into the nights going door to door to get the word out. The message of our mentors had been simple and direct: "There will be no excuses. Every man must stand for his children this one night. Just stand!" And stand they did.

As I was taking it all in, I was suddenly blinded by a flash of light. A reporter had snapped my picture. Just as Reverend Griffin had warned us, the white news media were there covering the story. I recognized one of the reporters from when he had tried to crash one of our private committee meetings. I saw another reporter who had written an article criticizing us for going outside of Farmville to have our grievances heard. At the time he wrote his article, all we wanted was for the school board to give us the new school they had been promising us for years. All we had wanted to do was correct a molehill. It was the local authorities who had turned it into a mountain. If they had dealt with the molehill, this huge turnout of the colored community could have been avoided, and they wouldn't have been faced with a demand for nonsegregation.

The NAACP lawyers who came to our assistance did not deal with molehills. Each had had considerable experience with civil rights issues. Each of them was as cool as a cucumber as he faced the crowd.

Reverend Griffin opened the meeting with a prayer and then turned it over to the lawyers and Barbara Johns, who spoke for our committee. They all were flawless. Each one had the full attention of the crowd. Even the buzzing outside the church quieted slightly. These formal presentations were followed by a question and answer period. Everything was going well until a former principal of Robert Russa Moton High School asked for permission to speak. A hush fell over the room. We all knew that he was a stooge—an ally—of Superintendent McIlwaine.

All heads in the room swiveled as he moved through the crowd to the center of the room. People literally held their breaths. We all knew he was going to set off fireworks, and he did not disappoint us. He not only criticized the strike and the strike leaders, he also had the nerve to berate and insult the superb group of lawyers who had agreed to take our case, accusing them of coming into our "quiet pastoral community" and disturbing the peace.

Mr. Lester Banks slowly approached the podium and started speaking. He ignored the stooge, choosing instead to speak directly to the crowd. He reminded them why we were gathered: To reaffirm our commitment to the vote for nonsegregation. As he headed back to his seat, Barbara Johns popped up as though shot out of a cannon. I had never seen her move so fast. She really lit into the stooge. She told the crowd to ignore him. Then she did two things that young people back then didn't dare do to adults. She raised her voice, and she called him an Uncle Tom—a traitor to his people. She crushed him with her words. When she finished, the former principal just turned and walked to the back of the room. I can still hear the thunderous ovation Barbara received when she finished her comments. I do believe that at that very moment her impromptu speech elevated her to another level in the eyes of our people. She was no longer just a 16-year-old student. She became a Superstar, an instant heroine. Her comments spoke volumes and profoundly reflected the feelings and frustrations of our community. Flashbulbs lit the room, and her picture was splashed on the front pages of newspapers all over the state.

The upshot of the meeting was that parents and students signed the petition for nonsegregation that had been drawn up by Martin A. Martin, Oliver W. Hill, and Spottswood W. Robinson, III. We had tears in our eyes as our parents signed, and we thanked them for their courage and support. When we collected all the copies of the petition that were circulating that night, we had nearly 200 signatures. We only needed one to file the lawsuit. The fact that so many people signed sent a strong message to the white power structure and, eventually, to the entire country and even the world. It was an amazing act of bravery during such a dangerous era. Those who signed knew they were risking life and limb. The lawyers told us that we could return to school on Monday morning, May 7. Then everyone headed home without incident.

The next day the press reported that our meeting had drawn the largest crowd of colored folks ever witnessed in that area except perhaps for the funeral of a respected person in our community. The press also declared that there had not been a single ounce of trouble. It probably didn't hurt that a military convoy from Camp Pickett, Virginia, had posted itself at Bush River, which is at the east entrance to Farmville on U.S. Route 460. Ironically, these troops were on the same route that General Grant had traveled as he chased General Lee into Farmville after defeating the Confederates at Sailor's Creek a century earlier.

The motors were kept idling on all the vehicles so they could be ready to move out at a moment's notice. This small Army task force included a fuel truck, four troop carriers, one vehicle with a machine gun turret, and the usual two jeeps, one in the front and one in the rear. The troops were equipped with ammunition, mustard gas, gas masks, and M-1 rifles with bayonets. They had a bazooka and two-way radios to summon back-up units if any were needed.

We heard later that both the extra law enforcement personnel and the soldiers had been called in by the local authorities because they were afraid the Ku Klux Klan and other opponents of black civil rights might try to disrupt our assembly. We suspected that the troops were really there more to protect the reputation of the white establishment than our safety. The oligarchy was smart. They wanted to be sure that outsiders saw them as the "good guys"—people who took care of their black people. Whatever the reason, it was a blessing for us. It had been a skittish night, but the result was a resounding victory. If the wolves, in fact, had been hovering, they claimed no victims—at least not that night.

CHAPTER 15

COVER ME

We were elated by the signing of the petition. At the same time, we were scared, and we had reason to be. Three weeks would go by between the signing of the petition on May 3 and the actual filing of the lawsuit in the Virginia court system by Spottswood W. Robinson, III on May 23, 1951. During this time, the white authorities approached a lot of parents including my own and asked them to take their names off the petition. The school board knew that if the petition process failed, it would get out from beneath a lawsuit.

Just three days after the petition was signed, our fears came to a head. On Sunday morning, May 6, my aunt Mary called to tell me that a cross was burning in the Moton schoolyard. I had heard about the Ku Klux Klan burning crosses across the Jim Crow South as a tactic to scare blacks, but I had never actually seen one. The cross on our school campus stood more than 10 feet high and was 7 feet across. It was made of green wood, so it did not burn well, but the kerosene-soaked rags that had been used to set the fire were still hanging from the cross. The colored community wanted the F.B.I. to investigate, but the local police dismissed the cross burning as just a prank. No one even remotely associated with law enforcement ever pursued the incident.

A photograph showing Thelma Allen, Admore Joyner, Rome Matthews, and me standing in front of the charred symbol of hate was published in the *Richmond Afro-American* newspaper on May 8, 1951. It was the only photograph of the incident ever published. Since white newspapers never covered the story, few if any whites heard about it. But I saw that symbol of hatred with my own eyes. It was a very frightening experience.

Living in the Jim Crow South was always scary for blacks, but tensions were running especially high in the aftermath of the strike and the petition signing. News of the cross burning spread like wildfire. The entire black community went into "cover me" mode. This meant that we protected ourselves and our loved ones from the threat of violence by arming ourselves. Because of the terror we felt, we kept loaded guns in our homes at all times. It even reached a point where there were no shotgun shells left to buy in the surrounding area.

We were ready to fight because we did not want a lynching or anything like that to take place. We had seen evidence of foul play in our community before, but no one had ever been killed or shot. We wanted to keep it that way. Colored boys who had moved up North to work sent word that they were on standby to come to Prince Edward County in case there was a conflict or confrontation between the coloreds and the whites. They were ready to leave their jobs and come down and fight beside their relatives if necessary. That's how serious the situation was during the time following the strike.

At my home, we kept five loaded guns ready. There was always a heightened sense of dread during the evening hours. Traditionally, that was when most incidents against blacks took place—under cover of darkness. I remember being afraid for our safety every time the barking of our dogs pierced the night quiet. As soon as we heard them, someone in the house would immediately turn out the lights, and another person would turn off the television. We operated in complete darkness. We had learned how to walk around the house without stumbling in the dark during World War II. Back then, blackouts were ordered every time the air-raid siren sounded at night. We could hear the wardens' vehicles moving up and down Route 15. They told everyone that if they saw any lights after the warning signal they would shoot in that direction. I am glad to say that never happened to us or to anyone we knew. Perhaps that was just some propaganda put out there to scare us, but we never tested the wardens to find out if it was true or not.

I recall one evening during the strike when the dogs were at a fever pitch, barking and baying. A car had pulled into our front yard. Daddy grabbed a loaded shotgun from the corner of the room and went out the back door. That door squeaked a bit, so we had to keep it greased. Otherwise the noise would alert whoever was out front that someone was coming up on his blind side. Daddy went around to the side of the house. Meanwhile, I listened for him to tap on the side of the house, signaling that he was in position. Just after I heard his tap, a person yelled out my mother's name. Mama recognized the voice as that of someone she did work for and quickly turned on the porch light. The person never knew that a 12-gauge shotgun had been aimed at him.

We don't know why no physical action was taken against blacks in the county during this stressful time, but I have always thanked God we were spared.

CHAPTER 16

DAVIS V. COUNTY SCHOOL BOARD OF PRINCE EDWARD COUNTY

Our strike ended on May 7, 1951, and the entire student body returned to school. In less than a month, Mr. Jones was fired as our principal. The Prince Edward County school authorities claimed they didn't fire him, they just terminated his job. To us, both actions had the same result. We collected hundreds of names on a petition aimed at keeping Mr. Jones as principal of Robert Russa Moton High School, but the white school officials wouldn't budge. John Lancaster was also fired as the county agent for the colored farmers. No longer would he be able to officially assist our community in raising better crops. Parents and students alike were upset about the firings. We saw these measures as retaliatory actions on the part of the white power structure, but we were powerless to do anything about them.

The day we had all worked for finally arrived on May 23, 1951, exactly one month after our strike began. Oliver W. Hill, Martin A. Martin, and Spottswood W. Robinson, III, of the NAACP filed a lawsuit against the Prince Edward County school district to integrate its schools. The case was called *Davis v. County School Board of Prince Edward County.* It was filed in the United States District Court for the Eastern District of Virginia, Richmond Division, where it was listed as Civil Action No. 1333. It was filed on behalf of 117 Robert Russa Moton High School students and 67 parents. The case name began with "Davis" because the first name on the list of student plaintiffs was Dorothy Davis, who was a ninth grader at my school. Her name was selected at random to be first. My sister and I were listed as "John Arthur Stokes and Carrie Stokes, infants, by Alice M. Stokes, their mother." All students were noted as "infants" even though we were all high school age.

What happened to all those names that were written on the petition at the First Baptist Church on the night of May 3? The complete list of names was published in the paper the day after the petition was signed. Just as you might suspect, various kinds of threats from the white power structure followed. Although the threat of physical harm was always there, most of the pressure was economic. It didn't make any difference if a person had signed the petition or not. All blacks in the county were targeted.

Some farmers discovered they could no longer sell their crops in Prince Edward County. Others had trouble getting credit from the banks. The situation became so bad for some that they were in danger of losing their homes, their farms, and their livelihoods. Those of us who ended up having our names listed as plaintiffs on the lawsuit were especially scared. On the day the suit was filed, fear prevailed even though we were ecstatic about taking legal action. We knew that the war had just begun. We were no longer fighting for something that was legally ours under the existing "separate but equal" clause that had been written into the U.S. Constitution after the *Plessy v. Ferguson* ruling in 1896. We were asking for whites and blacks to have the same educational opportunities in the same schools—together! We were challenging the Jim Crow system and a power structure that had been firmly in place in local, state, and national levels of government for centuries.

In 1953—two years after Carrie and I and most of the other strike leaders graduated—black students in Prince Edward County finally got a new high school, not because we won our case in court but because the white school board finally set aside the funds and built a new segregated school for black students. The new Robert Russa Moton High School was a state-of-the-art facility designed to accommodate 700 students. Our old high school (the brick building, not the tar-paper structures) became the Mary E. Branch Elementary School #2. Nothing was done, however, to improve any of the black elementary schools outside of Farmville. This meant that most young black children were still attending classes in one- and two-room wooden structures with wood or coal stoves and no indoor toilets or running water.

The white power structure was smart. They believed that if they could embarrass the NAACP by showing the world this state-of-the-art school for blacks and prove that they treated their black students as equals as the law required, the NAACP would have to withdraw its lawsuit. If that didn't work, they were sure that the courts would see that the county was abiding by the established law of separate but equal and rule in its favor. Either way, they would be the winners. In fact, the county did win the first round. In 1952 while the new high school was under construction, a three-judge panel of the U.S. District Court in Richmond unanimously rejected our request for nonsegregated schools. The court's decision was that the current school system had done no harm to either race!

That loss did not stop us. Three defense attorneys for the NAACP—Thurgood Marshall, James Nabrit, Jr., and Robert Carter—recommended combining the *Davis v. County School Board of Prince Edward County* case with four similar suits because the goal of each of them was desegregation of public schools. The other lawsuits had been filed in Delaware, South Carolina, Kansas, and the District of Columbia (Washington, D.C.). This is how our lawsuit came to be part of a class action suit called *Brown v. Board of Education.* Of the five suits that made up the new case, ours was the only one that had been student-led. The suit made it all the way to the U.S. Supreme Court where it was argued by Oliver W. Hill. The Court heard the five cases collectively because each challenged the doctrine of separate but equal and sought the same legal outcome.

On May 17, 1954, the decree was issued. The

U.S. Supreme Court justices unanimously ruled
that public school segregation was unconstitutional.
Chief Justice Earl Warren announced the decision:

> We come then to the question presented:
> Does segregation of children in public schools
> solely on the basis of race, even though the phys-
> ical facilities and other "tangible" factors may be
> equal, deprive the children of the minority
> group of equal educational opportunities?
> We believe that it does.
> We conclude that in the field of public
> education the doctrine of "separate but equal"
> has no place. Separate educational facilities are
> inherently unequal. Therefore, we hold that
> the plaintiffs and others similarly situated for
> whom the actions have been brought are, by
> reason of the segregation complained of,
> deprived of the equal protection of the laws
> guaranteed by the Fourteenth Amendment.

The landmark decision of *Brown v. Board of Education*
was filed on behalf of the students at Robert Russa
Moton High School and other colored children from
across our country who had to attend public schools

that were segregated. It was an important moment, but it was only the first step in overturning segregation in America.

CHAPTER 17

MASSIVE RESISTANCE

T he decision that segregation was unconstitutional stunned the nation. You
might think that state leaders and their
national representatives would have followed the new
ruling and immediately begun the process of deseg-
regating schools. But the complete opposite happened in countless locations. Many states, especially
those in the Jim Crow South, resisted the ruling.

On April 11–14, 1955, the Supreme Court justices
heard arguments on the question of how desegregation was to be achieved. Chief Justice Earl Warren
announced the ruling of the Court on May 31, 1955.
He stated that the cases that made up *Brown v. Board of
Education* were decided on May 17, 1954. The decision
of *Brown II,* as the new case was called, upheld that
racial discrimination in public education was

unconstitutional. But in their new ruling, the justices delegated the task of desegregation to local school authorities and to district courts. The order to these courts was that desegregation of public schools should occur "with all deliberate speed." Many people who supported equal rights were upset with the new mandate. They believed that the order did not convey the urgency of the first *Brown* decision and would open the way for all sorts of delays in implementing the new law. In other words, life would go on as usual in the Jim Crow South.

That is exactly what happened. Little or no movement toward desegregation took place in the South. In fact, it was common for Southern white legislators and school board members to enact laws and policies that openly defied the U.S. Supreme Court's *Brown* ruling. This movement became known as Massive Resistance. Furthermore, most congressmen from the Jim Crow South signed a decree called the "Southern Manifesto." That document stated that *Brown v. Board of Education* was an abuse of judicial power. The state government leaders argued that our national government had no power to force the integration of public schools within the states. The 101 signers of the "Southern Manifesto" pledged to use the law to overturn *Brown v. Board of Education* on the grounds that it was unconstitutional.

The Commonwealth of Virginia was a leading supporter of Massive Resistance. The Commission on Public Education reported that separate facilities were educationally sound and were in the best interest of both races. The state legislators who served on the commission also urged school officials across the state to stand firm against mandatory integration. They threatened to close schools rather than require any child to attend a nonsegregated school.

Harry F. Byrd of Virginia was one of the members of the United States Senate who authored and signed the "Southern Manifesto" and its "Declaration of Constitutional Principles." Byrd was governor of Virginia from 1926 through 1930 and represented Virginia in the U.S. Senate from 1933 until 1965. During the period after the *Brown* decision, Byrd was one of the most vocal supporters of maintaining policies of racial segregation. On the day of the landmark decision, Byrd warned that the ruling would bring dangers of the greatest consequence and would create problems that had not been confronted before in our nation.

Senator Byrd was extremely powerful in Virginia

politics for many years. It was said that his "nod," or approval, was necessary before a candidate could win any office, including that of governor. Under Byrd's influence, government officials withheld state funding for the integration of schools. His "Byrd Machine" preserved the Jim Crow lifestyle in Virginia for years after *Brown.*

Following Byrd's lead, the Board of Supervisors of Prince Edward County voted to stop the funding for public schools in the county. A strictly segregated public school system was maintained until 1959. That's when the courts finally ruled that the county's schools had to desegregate. In an amazing act of defiance, the Board of Supervisors voted to close all of the county's public schools—white as well as black—rather than integrate the system. All public schools in the county remained closed from 1959 to 1964. That's five years!

No one could attend any public school for the sole reason that the white power structure wanted to maintain segregated facilities rather than desegregate them. It should come as no surprise that during this period, the white power structure came up with a way to make it possible for white children to attend school. They created private schools and gave countless white children vouchers that could be used to help pay the cost of attending these schools. Money poured in from segregationists all around the country to help pay for these schools. No vouchers were ever provided to colored children. Since they were barred from attending the white private schools and all the black schools were closed, they were denied the opportunity to get an education in the county.

Signs reading "School Property, No Trespassing Under Penalty of Law, Prince Edward County School Board" were posted in the front yards of schools. Almost all of the county's 1,700 colored students missed five years of their education. The same was true for poor white children. Think about it! Children who were 6 years old in 1959 were 11 before the schools reopened. This made for some interesting classrooms with a broad range of ages. Some students missed their entire high school years, which meant going to college was out of the question. Jobs were difficult to get without a high school diploma. These children have been referred to as the "lost generation."

Some colored children who were fortunate enough to have family members living outside of Prince Edward County were able to attend schools in other areas. However, these students had to live miles away from home, their parents, and their siblings. A religious group called the Quakers made it possible for some high school students to live with host families in Pennsylvania, New Jersey, and a few other northern states. This gave them the opportunity to complete their high school education and get a diploma. Some of these students went on to find careers that they might never have considered if they had stayed in Prince Edward County.

Its shameful act of resistance made Prince Edward County the only county in the entire United States to deny students access to public education for such an extended time solely for the purpose of avoiding school desegregation. In September 1964 another U.S. Supreme Court ruling forced the reopening of all public schools in Prince Edward County. Reverend Griffin, the same leader who had supported us in our student strike in 1951, initiated the case of *Griffin v. County School Board of Prince Edward County* in which he challenged the closing of the county's public schools. As a result, publicly funded schools in the county were officially desegregated between 1964 and 1965. In reality, however, the process continued over a much longer period of time. Full integration did not occur until the 1980s.

STANDING ON SHOULDERS

I was only 19 years old when my sister, my schoolmates, and I embarked on the path that—despite tremendous obstacles—eventually ended the separate and unequal educational conditions for African American students not only in Prince Edward County but also in the entire country. Because we had the courage and determination to strike for equality and the promise of social justice for all, we made a difference. Even though we were only high school students, we knew we had to press forward. By doing so, we brought about social change. Had we faltered, God only knows what the result would have been in Farmville, Virginia, the Jim Crow South, and even the country as a whole.

The rulings of *Brown I* in 1954 and *Brown II* in 1955 are among the most important decisions of the

U.S. Supreme Court because they declared the concept of separate but equal schools unconstitutional and forced all jurisdictions to cease segregation. Why, then, don't people know much about the role of our student strike in the *Brown v. Board of Education* cases? Why did I wait 50 years to write about what went on at Robert Russa Moton High School?

Partly it was because of the vow of secrecy the strike committee took not to reveal the names of anyone who was involved in the planning, but also it is because for more than half a century I have had to deal with a lot of hurt connected to that event—things that are painful for me to think about. You see, many of the people who were denied an education when the schools were closed from 1959 to 1964 blamed the Moton students— especially those who were plaintiffs in the case that became part of *Brown v. Board of Education*—for what they suffered as a result of not being able to go to school. The school closings affected their chances to get decent jobs, which in turn impacted their chances for future success. Many of these people were very bitter. I didn't want to do anything that might stir up more resentment or make life difficult for my family.

I am speaking now because I realize our student strike was one of the events that drastically changed

American education and was a catalyst to the modern civil rights movement. It deserves to be remembered. Many of the key players cannot speak for themselves because they are already gone.

It is important for people to know whose shoulders the students of Robert Russa Moton High School stood on—people like Reverend Griffin, Oliver W. Hill, Lester Banks, and of course our brothers and sisters, and our parents and teachers. I particularly want all young people today to understand whose shoulders you are standing on or should be standing on. It is important for you to realize that you did not get where you are by yourselves. The best way to get an understanding of self is to know where you came from and where you are going.

I want to make it clear how important it is for you to not get discouraged. Instead, set an example for your fellow students. If you do, then one day someone will be able to stand on your shoulders. If not, the struggle of those who came before you may be in vain. As Oliver W. Hill said, "Don't feel powerless; you can change the world."

I live by a concept from the Bible found in Galatians 5:1, which says that we should never permit another generation to grow up in bondage. To me, not teaching others about the five individual cases—particularly the Prince Edward County, Virginia, case—that led to *Brown v. Board of Education* would make me feel that I have failed to follow the mandates of the Bible. The story behind *Davis v. County School Board of Prince Edward County* must get into the history books so that the struggle of the Robert Russa Moton High School students will continue to live on long after we have all passed from the face of this Earth. We were given a charge to stand up for equality and justice for all people. We have to be certain that we keep that charge alive. That is my goal. We must never back down. I want to plant this seed in the mind of every person, young and old.

What happened to me after the student strike? What have I done to contribute to the betterment of society? Let me bring you up to date on a few things that I haven't mentioned about my life. I graduated from Robert Russa Moton High School in June 1951. In the fall I returned to the campus as a "post-graduate" student. I wanted to go to college but couldn't at the time. Daddy was in the hospital, so I had to stay home to help Mama. Hampden-Sydney College was just a few miles from my home in Kingsville. However, at the time that institution was only open to white males. The nearest college for colored students—Saint Paul's College—was 50 miles away in Lawrenceville, Virginia. That was too far to go and still be able to take care of the farm. There were a lot of other young black men in the same predicament as I was, including those who came out of the Army after World War II.

It was as if the white man had erected a mountain as a huge stumbling block in front of us, and we had to figure out how to tunnel through it—how to over-come all the obstacles we faced—in order to get to the other side. Well, that's exactly what we did. We knew that education and knowledge were power. We had patience, and we endured. Thus, while returning to high school to take classes after having graduated from that same school may seem really odd to you, "separate but equal" gave us no other choice.

By the end of the school year, Daddy was back at work on the farm. I left Moton and served in the Army for two years. From 1954 to 1959 I was enrolled in Virginia State University where my major was elementary education. I began my teaching career in Portsmouth, Virginia, then moved to Maryland, where I got a job with the Baltimore City Public Schools. I worked as a teacher and in time became a

master teacher and a Rockefeller Foundation Scholar.
Eventually, I left the classroom to become an admin-
istrative assistant to the superintendent, an educational specialist, a vice principal, and ultimately, a principal of the Frankford Intermediate School on the east
side of Baltimore. After 30 years in education, I
retired and started lecturing on the Prince Edward
County, Virginia, case in the landmark *Brown v. Board
of Education* decision.

In October 1996 Robert Russa Moton High
School was added to the National Register of Historic
Places, and in August 1998 it was designated a
National Historic Landmark by the U.S. Secretary
of the Interior. Imagine, the actions of Barbara
Johns, my twin sister, Carrie, and I, along with the
other Manhattan Project leaders and Robert Russa
Moton High School students of 1951 have made our
alma mater so important that it has become a part
of the National Park Service! The records and documents that commemorate the student strike of April
23, 1951, are on display there for the whole world
to see. If you were to visit this historic site, would
you be able to see the tar-paper structures of 1951?
No, they are gone, but you could see photos of those
leaky, smelly facilities.

In 2008 the Virginia Civil Rights Memorial is scheduled to be dedicated. I am proud to say that our efforts will be the subject of one of its panels. The memorial will stand on the grounds of the Virginia state capitol building in Richmond for visitors from every state and nation to see.

Efforts are now being made to atone for the mistakes made in Prince Edward County, Virginia. The General Assembly of Virginia has established a *Brown v. Board of Education* Scholarship Awards Program. Two million dollars have been set aside to provide financial aid to residents of Virginia—blacks and whites—who were enrolled in public schools between 1959 and 1964 in systems that closed schools rather than desegregate them. Of course, Prince Edward County, which had the longest school closure, is included in those systems. The establishment of this fund is due in large part to a series of rallies called "Get on the Bus," which were the brainchild of my friend Ken Woodley, editor of the *Farmville Herald*. Ironically, this is the same newspaper that was against us during the strike. I had the honor of being a spokesperson for the program. Thanks to Virginia Delegate Viola Baskerville, House Bill 846, which eventually created the scholarship fund, was introduced in the state General Assembly. Because of it, members of the state legislature were forced to face issues from the past and right the wrongs. Because they did, many people throughout the state of Virginia are now recipients of these funds, and a few just graduated from college.

Throughout my years, I have always championed education. As a student, teacher, principal, and life-long educator, I have consistently tried to treat others with dignity, respect, and fairness. I live by the lessons I learned from Mrs. LaVerne R. Pervall, one of my favorite teachers. She taught me speech, English, writing, literature, and how to be an orator—how to capture the imagination of my audience. Words from a poem she introduced me to long ago have helped guide me through life. Perhaps they will do the same for you.

Look not at the face
nor the color of a person's skin,
but look at the heart
which is deep within.
For the face and the skin
will one day fade away,
but the deeds of a good person
will never decay.

BIBLIOGRAPHY

To write *Students on Strike* I relied mainly on my memory of
the events; the diary my sister Carrie kept as secretary of our
Manhattan Project; my high school yearbook; conversations
with family members, friends, and other participants in
the strike; newspaper articles, especially those published in
the *Farmville Herald,* the *Richmond Times-Dispatch,* the *Richmond
Afro-American,* and the *Roanoke Times;* and the books and Web
sites listed under Resources on the opposite page. Below are
some additional sources.

Bradshaw, Herbert Clarence. *History of Prince Edward County,*
Virginia. Richmond, Virginia: Dietz Press, Incorporated,
1955, 2003.

_____. *Brown v. Board of Education: Virginia's Role and Response.*
Richmond, Virginia: Dr. Martin Luther King, Jr., Memorial
Commission.

Davis Versus Board of Education Prince Edward County, Farmville, Virginia.
Civil Action #1333, filed on 23 May 1951.

McCormick, Peter. "How a Band of High School Students
Influenced Desegregation." Published in *The College Board
Review,* No. 200, pp. 34–39, Fall 2004.

Interview with Tavis Smiley
http://www.npr.org/news/specials/brown50/

RESOURCES

BOOKS

Kluger, Richard. *Simple Justice: The History of* Brown v. Board of Education *and Black America's Struggle for Equality.* NY: Knopf, 1975 (first edition); Vintage Books, 2004.

Smith, Bob. *They Closed Their Schools.* Chapel Hill, NC: The University of North Carolina Press, 1965.

WEB SITES

Voices of Freedom, Virginia Commonwealth University
www.library.vcu.edu/jbc/speccoll/civilrights.html#list
See the commitment on his face and hear the passion in his voice as John A. Stokes comments on his role in the movement for equal rights in this collection of oral histories.

Dr. Edward H. Peeples
www.library.vcu.edu/jbc/speccoll/pec.html
Explore segregation in Prince Edward County, Virginia, through photographs and documents that reveal the disparity between black and white schools.

Virginia Center for Digital History
www.vcdh.virginia.edu/HIST604/davisgallery/index.html
Compare the 124 photographs that were filed in the Davis v. County School Board of Prince Edward County *case that depicted exteriors and interiors of Prince Edward County public schools.*

The Robert Russa Moton Museum
www.motonmuseum.com/news.html
Find current articles related to the museum's past, present, and future.

Founded in 1888, the National Geographic Society is one of the largest nonprofit scientific and educational organizations in the world. It reaches more than 285 million people worldwide each month through its official journal, NATIONAL GEOGRAPHIC, and its four other magazines; the National Geographic Channel; television documentaries; radio programs; films; books; videos and DVDs; maps; and interactive media. National Geographic has funded more than 8,000 scientific research projects and supports an education program combating geographic illiteracy.

For more information, please call 1-800-NGS LINE (647-5463) or write to the following address:
National Geographic Society,
1145 17th Street N.W., Washington, D.C.
20036-4688 U.S.A.

Visit us online at www.nationalgeographic.com/books